A Shelter Sketchbook

JEN —

IT'S BEEN GREAT TO RECONNECT,
AND I THINK YOU'RE DOING EXCELLENT —
AND TREMENDOUSLY VALUABLE — WORK AT
CSC.

THIS BOOK HIGHLIGHTS A HOST
OF TIMELESS COMMONSENSE BUILDING
IDEAS THAT COULD CERTAINLY CON-
TRIBUTE TO THE PRACTICALITY AND
SUSTAINABILITY OF TODAY'S (AND
TOMORROW'S) BUILT ENVIRONMENT.
I HOPE YOU FIND IT OF INTEREST.

WARMEST REGARDS,

JOHN (STAN)
2/15/13

JOHN S. TAYLOR

A Shelter Sketchbook

Timeless Building Solutions

CHELSEA GREEN PUBLISHING COMPANY

WHITE RIVER JUNCTION, VERMONT

Printed in the United States of America

1 2 3 4 5   97 98 99 00 01

First Chelsea Green edition: July, 1997

Originally published under the title *Commonsense Architecture* by W.W. Norton & Co. in the U.S.
and by George J. McLeod, Ltd. in Canada.

Library of Congress Cataloging-in-Publication Data

Taylor, John S., 1947–
[Commonsense architecture]
A shelter sketchbook : timeless building solutions / John S. Taylor
p. cm.
Originally published: Commonsense architecture. New York : Norton.
c 1983
Includes bibliographical references (p.) and index.
ISBN 1-890132-02-0 (pbk.)
1. Vernacular architecture. I. Title.
NA208.T39 1997   97-28509
720—dc21   CIP

Chelsea Green Publishing Company
P.O. Box 428
White River Junction, VT 05001

To my mother, who ignited my interest in design,
and to the innumerable anonymous builders who fanned that flame
with their wonderfully creative and pragmatic spirit.

I WOULD LIKE TO ACKNOWLEDGE the assistance of Jim Mairs, my editor at W.W. Norton, whose shared enthusiasm for the wisdom to be gained from exploring folk architecture made the first edition possible. I would also like to thank Etsuko Penner, Clee and Suzanne Edgar, Pan American Airlines, and the government of Japan for their assistance in facilitating much of my research. Thanks also to Walter Paine for his appreciation of this work, and for motivating me to pursue its republication, and to Jim Schley, Stephen Morris, and Ian Baldwin of Chelsea Green for making that goal a reality. The careful and creative work by the entire staff at Chelsea Green has resulted in a high-quality book with many improvements over the first edition, such as the extremely valuable comprehensive index.

Finally, I would like to thank my family and friends for their support and input, and most especially my partner, Gail, for her encouragement and patience in helping me bring this work back to life.

Contents

Preface to the Second Edition

"When one has completed the necessary. . . one immediately comes upon the beautiful and the pleasing."

—Voltaire

THROUGH THE COURSE OF HISTORY, indigenous architecture has been shaped primarily by three factors:

environmental impacts—climate, geography, and wildlife, including pests and predators;
available resources—building materials, as well as energy and skilled labor;
human needs—the space required for specific uses.

In the post–energy-crisis years of the late 1970s, many people were actively searching for ways to create more practical and efficient buildings. The publication of the first edition of this book, under the title *Commonsense Architecture*, represented an effort to expose readers to a vast reservoir of useful and innovative design ideas: the accumulated wisdom of anonymous folk builders from around the world. Happily, in recent years there has been—for environmental, economic, ethical, and simply pragmatic reasons—a resurgence of interest in constructing buildings that are more respectful of the three factors mentioned above. In response to this renewed interest the book is being reissued to offer up, once again, a host of timeless ideas that can be of great benefit to anyone involved in design or building today.

Most studies of architecture focus on the evolution of this discipline as it has been shaped by a fourth, admittedly very powerful influence—culture: the combined effects of beliefs, superstitions, social structures, conventions, and fashions. The influences of both human needs and culture upon architecture are complex. Certainly the culture shapes the buildings, and in many ways the buildings then exert a profound influence on the culture. The strength of this connection can be heard in the Kickapoo saying, "By our houses you will know us," as cited by Peter Nabokov in *Native American Architecture* (Oxford, 1989).

Unfortunately, in developing a more culture-oriented view of architecture, we have often obscured the principle of pragmatism behind a veil of style. Elements are frequently appreciated more for appearance than for practicality and purpose. Efficiency is often sacrificed for the sake of an architectural "statement," leaving us with an ever-expanding need to rely upon technological interventions and the consumption of valuable resources.

The process that led to the creation of this book began almost twenty years ago with an investigation into the origins of passive solar design. It quickly became clear that many of the principles and practices being employed in contemporary solar design were centuries old. It was also very obvious that in this respect the question of passive solar was not unique, but was just one of a huge number of practical building considerations that had been addressed by our ancestors with the mindful application of ingenuity and common sense. Ancient builders throughout the world consistently displayed a strong connection with their surrounding environment, a deep understanding of the available resources, and a keen awareness of human needs. These perspectives shaped the development of all successful indigenous architectures throughout the ages.

The primary objective of *A Shelter Sketchbook* is to refocus attention on those three perspectives. The following illustrations of indigenous folk architecture from around the globe highlight ways in which the unselfconscious utilization of common sense can yield elegantly simple, practical, and timeless solutions to the most basic needs addressed by human shelters. The hundreds of pen-and-ink drawings chronicle an architecture that makes sense, not simply a statement. The first section of the book illustrates how buildings respond to external environmental factors such as climate and predators. The second section describes ways in which various activities such as sleeping and cooking are accommodated within dwellings. And the final section investigates the materials and construction practices used to build shelters.

The ultimate goal of *A Shelter Sketchbook* is to improve the quality of our contemporary built environment by helping inspire people to value and use a vast, rich, and often untapped resource: the practical wisdom embodied in folk architecture. This book represents an effort to replace a growing dependency upon precious resources with an increased reliance upon resourcefulness.

Section I - protection from the Environment

Nature as provider of Shelter

Shelters evolved to give protection from the hostile aspects of the environment, primarily harsh weather and threats from other animals. For eons tree-dwelling apes have constructed crude leaf and twig platforms in the trees to raise themselves above the dangers on the ground and to partially ward off the rain and hot sun.

Chimpanzee in sleeping platform

Arboreal jungle tent used in a biological research program Amazon Jungle, 1980

People have continued this practice of rising above dangers by constructing aerie fortresses.

Metéora, Greece

Appropriate siting can greatly reduce unwanted environmental impacts. Elevation, orientation, and wind protection are carefully considered by both animals and traditional indigenous builders.

SUN

WIND

COOL AIR

MOST PRIMITIVE DWELLINGS SHOW
A STRONG SENSITIVITY TO LOCAL
CONDITIONS. OUT OF NECESSITY THEY
TAKE MAXIMUM ADVANTAGE OF
THE NATURAL AMENITIES TO
GAIN INCREASED COMFORT
AND PROTECTION.

CLIFF DWELLINGS
MESA VERDE,
COLORADO

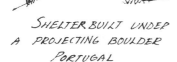

SHELTER BUILT UNDER
A PROJECTING BOULDER
PORTUGAL

WHERE CONDITIONS WERE
RIGHT, BUILDERS OFTEN CHOSE
TO CREATE SHELTERS BY
CARVING THEM OUT OF
THE EARTH.

DWELLINGS PARTLY CUT
INTO CLIFFS AND PARTLY
BUILT OUT FROM THEM
SETENIL, SPAIN

ELABORATE FACADES WERE
ADDED TO MANY
DWELLINGS CARVED OUT
OF SOFT STONE CLIFFS.
TOURAINE, FRANCE

FOR MILLIONS OF YEARS MANY ANIMALS
HAVE USED UNDERGROUND SANCTUARIES
FOR PROTECTION FROM COLD, HEAT, RAIN,
SNOW, PREDATORS, ETC. EARLY MAN
LEARNED A GREAT DEAL ABOUT
SHELTERS FROM THE OTHER ANIMALS
AND SAW THE
VALUE OF THE
BURROWED
HOME.

SMALL ANT COLONY

DWELLINGS
HOLLOWED OUT
OF NATURAL CONES
OF POROUS LIMESTONE,
OR TUFA.

CAPPADOCIA, TURKEY

NORTH

FRONT VIEW AND PLAN OF HOUSES CUT
OUT OF A VOLCANIC STONE, CALLED TUFF, IN MASSAFRA,
ITALY. THE FAN-SHAPED ROOMS
LEFT A MINIMAL HOLE IN THE
FACE OF THE FRAGILE ROCK
AND HAD NO DARK
CORNERS.

HOUSE DUG INTO ROCK
CONE COMPLETE WITH
A FINISHED FACADE
AND A CHIMNEY

GUADIX, SPAIN

DWELLINGS
DUG OUT
OF SOFT
LOESS SOIL
AND RADIATING
FROM A SUNKEN
CENTRAL COURT.
(NORTHERN CHINA)

PLAN VIEW

THE SUNKEN COURT
CONCEPT IS
STILL USED
EFFECTIVELY
TODAY.

JOHN BARNARD'S
ECOLOGY HOUSE
OSTERVILLE,
MASSACHUSETTS

SOME EARTH - SHELTERED
HOMES ARE DUG INTO
A HILL SO THAT ONLY
ONE WALL (USUALLY TO
THE SOUTH) IS
EXPOSED FOR
ACCESS AND LIGHT.

BANKED HOUSE, AMERICAN
MIDWEST

IN HIS COOP HOMESTEAD
PLANS IN 1942, FRANK
LLOYD WRIGHT PROPOSED
SHELTERING THE HOUSE
WITH AN EARTH BERM.

STAYING DRY

Offering protection from the rain is a primary goal for shelters in most climates.

Hut on Alor Island near Borneo

This simple shelter serves as both a rain hat and sun shade.

House on Flores Island

The steep thatch roof is designed to shed the heavy Indonesian rains.

METAL

THATCH

Japanese House

The metal cap along the peak of the roof protects this often leaky spot in thatch roofs.

Hay Storage Shed, Holland

As hay is added the roof is raised with ropes from the poles. The roof sheds the rain, while air can still get in to dry the hay.

Early Greek House

Covered interior balconies create living spaces out of the sun and rain.

THE SMALL HIP SEGMENT ON THIS GABLE ROOF PROTECTS A SMALL PORCH THAT CAN BE USED IN ALL WEATHER AS A PLACE TO WORK AND TO DRY FOOD AND CLOTHES.

COVERED PORCH
ON LAKE GENEVA, SWITZERLAND

THIS HOUSE IN NORTHWEST NEW GUINEA NOT ONLY GIVES GOOD PROTECTION FROM THE HEAVY RAINS BUT ALSO INSURES COOLING THROUGH-VENTILATION.

KAMBOT HOUSE
SEPIK, NORTHEAST NEW GUINEA

SMALL ROOFS, HOODS, AND CANTILEVERED OVERHANGS ARE ALSO VERY EFFECTIVE DEVICES FOR DIVERTING THE RAIN.

DOOR HOOD ON
PENNSYLVANIA
FARMHOUSE

PENTICE, OR PENT ROOF,
ON A BARN IN
PENNSYLVANIA

CANTILEVERED
OUTSHOT ON
BARN IN
DELAWARE

HERE THE OVER-HANGING UPPER FLOOR ACTS AS A RAIN HOOD FOR LOWER LEVEL.

IN AREAS WHERE FRESH WATER WAS
A VERY LIMITED COMMODITY MANY
INNOVATIVE SYSTEMS EVOLVED FOR
THE COLLECTION AND STORAGE
OF RAINWATER.

FIELD SHELTER
SOUTHERN ITALY

THE FLAT ROOF IS USED FOR
DRYING CROPS AND THE PLASTER DOWNSPOUT
CARRIES RAINWATER TO A CISTERN (1600)

GUTTERS AND DOWNSPOUTS ARE
THE MAIN TOOLS FOR
WATER COLLECTION:

JAPANESE SLUNG BAMBOO
GUTTER SERVING TWO ROOFS

JAPANESE
WOOD AND
BAMBOO
DOWNSPOUT
(1700's)

JAPANESE BAMBOO
GUTTER AND DOWNSPOUT
HUNG FROM METAL
BRACKETS
(1659)

LOG GUTTER
FORT CLATSOP,
OREGON
(1805)

17

SECTION

CISTERN

PLAN

IMPLUVIUM

CISTERN

BENIN HOUSE
SOUTHERN NIGERIA

THE CENTRAL COURT-
YARD, OR IMPLUVIUM,
ACTS AS A RAINWATER
COLLECTION BASIN THAT
EMPTIES INTO A CISTERN
BURRIED AT ONE
CORNER.

THE STONE TRULLO
DWELLINGS IN APULIA,
ITALY OFTEN HAVE
DOWNSPOUTS THAT CARRY
RAINWATER INTO LARGE, ROOFED
CISTERNS. THIS WATER IS
USED BOTH FOR DRINKING
AND FOR WATERING
CROPS.

LIVING
SPACE

CISTERN

IN THE AMERICAN WEST, THE
CUSTOMARY WATER BARREL WAS A
AN ABOVE-GROUND CISTERN
FOR RAINWATER.

PUEBLO DWELLING
ROOF

SCUPPER

SUDDEN RAINS
IN THE AMERICAN
SOUTHWEST ARE
QUICKLY DRAINED
FROM THE FLAT EARTH
ROOFS BY SCUPPERS THAT
USUALLY DIRECT THE WATER INTO BARRELS.

LIVING SPACE

CZECHOSLOVAKIAN HOUSE
THE GABLE WALL IS
PROTECTED BY A ROOF
PROJECTION AND A
CANTILEVERED, OR
JETTIED, SECOND FLOOR.

SIDE VIEW

PROTECTING THE WALLS OF
THE HOUSE FROM THE RAIN
IS IMPORTANT FOR THEIR PRE-
SERVATION, AND VARIOUS
DESIGN ELEMENTS HAVE
EVOLVED TO MEET
THIS NEED.

THE JETTIED GABLE PRO-
TECTS THE END WALL BELOW,
THE LARGE ROOF OVERHANG
PROTECTS THE FRONT SECOND-
FLOOR WALL, AND THE
CANTILEVERED, OR GARRISONED,
SECOND FLOOR PROTECTS THE
FRONT WALL OF THE FIRST FLOOR.

PAUL REVERE'S HOUSE
BOSTON, MASSACHUSETTS
(BUILT IN 1660)

MEXICAN HOUSE
NEAR HIDALGO
THE FANNED GABLE OF
HAND-SPLIT SHAKES PROTECTS
THE SOFT MUD BRICK
WALL BELOW.

COTTAGE
CAMBRIDGESHIRE, ENGLAND
THE SLOPING PENTICE
BOARDS PROTECT THE GABLE WALL.

SIFNOS ISLAND, GREECE

PLASTER OVER THESE ROUGH STONE WALLS PROTECTS THE SOFT MASONRY.

MASONRY WALLS ARE PARTICULARLY VULNERABLE TO DETERIORATION WHEN EXPOSED TO MOISTURE, SO THEY REQUIRE SPECIAL PROTECTION.

FIELD WALL, GREECE
THE PLASTER CAP PROTECTS THE STONEWORK BELOW.

PARAPET WALL, MEXICO

SLOPING TILES KEEP THE RAIN FROM EATING AWAY THE SOFT MUD BRICK WALLS.

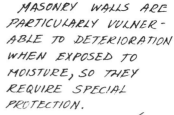

MEDIEVAL WINDOW ENGLAND

THE DRIP BAND AROUND THE UPPER SIDE OF THE WINDOW PREVENTS WATER FROM FLOWING DOWN THE WALL AND INTO THE SASH AND SILL JOINTS.

DRIP COURSE ENGLAND

THE PROJECTING COURSE OF BRICKS KEEPS WATER FROM FLOWING DOWN THE WALL AND DAMAGING THE MASONRY.

LACKING MODERN FLASHING MATERIALS, EARLY BUILDERS IN WALES RELIED ON PROJECTING SLATES TO KEEP THE RAIN AWAY FROM THE ROOF / WALL JUNCTION.

PROJECTING LOGGIA, ST. AUGUSTINE, FLORIDA (1700's)
THE SLOPED FLOOR PREVENTS STANDING WATER FROM ROTTING THE FLOOR.

BANNISTER JOINT, ST. AUGUSTINE, FLORIDA (1700's)

THE V-JOINT KEEPS WATER FROM COLLECTING IN THE JOINT AND ROTTING THE WOOD.

PORCH POST, VIRGINIA (1800's)
THE METAL BASE PROTECTS THE POST FROM WATER THAT RUNS OFF THE PORCH.

STONE SCUPPERS KEEP THE WATER OFF THE PLASTERED WALLS OF THE STONE TRULLO.

STONE TRULLO APULIA, ITALY (1600's)

JAPANESE GUTTER AND DOWNSPOUT

THE WATER FLOWS ALONG THE CHAINS TO THE GRAVEL BED BELOW AND DOESN'T SPLASH THE HOUSE WALL.

GRAVEL BED

JAPANESE FENCE POST (1600's)
THE BASE IS STONE TO RESIST ROT AND THE UPPER PART IS WOOD.

PARASOL ROOF
WITHOUT WALLS,
SAMOA

IF WATER VAPOR IS ALLOWED TO
CONDENSE ON WOOD OR OTHER
PLANT BUILDING MATERIALS IT
WILL CAUSE MILDEW AND ROT.
A VARIETY OF TECHNIQUES
CAN PREVENT THIS.

IN HOT, HUMID AREAS IT IS
IMPORTANT TO PROMOTE GOOD
FLOW-THROUGH VENTILATION
TO PREVENT
CONDENSATION.

OPEN REED WALL,
MADAGASCAR

ALPINE BARN
(1818)

THE OPEN CONSTRUCTION OF
THE EXTERIOR HAY MOW PRO-
TECTED BY THE DEEP ROOF
OVERHANG ALLOWS FOR AIR
FLOW TO DRY THE HAY.

AS MOIST AIR PASSES
THROUGH A WALL FROM
THE WARM SIDE TO THE
COLD SIDE, IT MAY REACH
ITS DEW POINT AND CON-
DENSE WITHIN THE WALL,
CAUSING MILDEW AND ROT.
VAPOR BARRIERS IN
MODERN HOMES ARE IN-
STALLED TO STOP THE
MOISTURE BEFORE IT
GETS INTO THE WALL.

WALL SECTION:

ROT CAUSED BY
CONDENSATION IN A
COOL, MOIST CRAWL-
SPACE IS CURBED
WITH FOUNDATION
VENTS.

SLIDING VENT,
QUEBEC

COLD SIDE
DEW POINT
INSULATION
WARM
SIDE

VAPOR
BARRIER
(THIN
PLASTIC
FILM)

PROTECTION FROM THE WIND

HOUSE FORMS THAT OFFER LITTLE AIR RESISTANCE AND CREATE NO TURBULENCE REDUCE THE STRUCTURAL AND THERMAL IMPACTS OF THE WIND.

WIND

WIND OVER THE RECTANGULAR HOUSE CREATES TURBULENT EDDIES, WHILE THE WIND FLOWS EVENLY OVER THE SEMICIRCULAR ONE.

WIND

LEAN-TO WIND SHELTER AKSEHIR, TURKEY

THE HOUSE BELOW HAS A ROOF SHAPED LIKE A BOAT'S HULL THAT HAS ITS BOW TURNED INTO THE WIND.

WIND

NORMANDY FARMHOUSE

NEW ENGLAND SALTBOX
(1800's)

THE SALTBOX HOUSES OF NEW ENGLAND LET THE COLD NORTH WINDS GLIDE OVER THE LONG, SLOPING ROOF.

THE TERRAIN AROUND THIS CONTEMPORARY EARTH-SHELTERED HOME IS CONTOURED TO CREATE A MINIMUM OF AIR TURBULENCE.

THE BACKSTRIP BY THIS ARAB
TENT BREAKS THE HOT,
SANDY DESERT WINDS.

INUIT IGLOOS
OFTEN HAD A WIND-
SCREEN WALL BY THE
ENTRANCE

ROCKY MOUNTAIN
TEPEE WITH
WIND SCREEN

EARLY JAPANESE BUILDERS
OFTEN PLACED STONES
ON THE WOOD SHINGLES
TO PREVENT THE WIND
FROM BLOWING THEM OFF.

IN IRELAND, A ROPE NET WEIGHTED WITH
STONES SECURES THE THATCH.

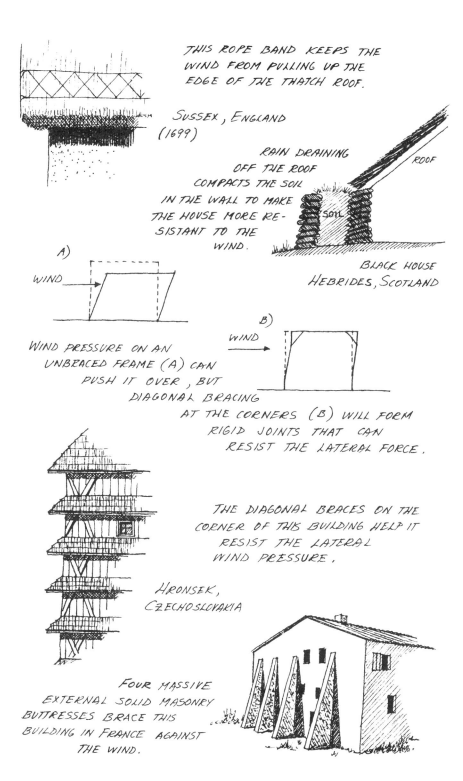

THIS ROPE BAND KEEPS THE WIND FROM PULLING UP THE EDGE OF THE THATCH ROOF.

SUSSEX, ENGLAND (1699)

RAIN DRAINING OFF THE ROOF COMPACTS THE SOIL IN THE WALL TO MAKE THE HOUSE MORE RE-SISTANT TO THE WIND.

ROOF

SOIL

BLACK HOUSE HEBRIDES, SCOTLAND

A)

WIND

B)

WIND

WIND PRESSURE ON AN UNBRACED FRAME (A) CAN PUSH IT OVER, BUT DIAGONAL BRACING AT THE CORNERS (B) WILL FORM RIGID JOINTS THAT CAN RESIST THE LATERAL FORCE.

THE DIAGONAL BRACES ON THE CORNER OF THIS BUILDING HELP IT RESIST THE LATERAL WIND PRESSURE.

HRONSEK, CZECHOSLOVAKIA

FOUR MASSIVE EXTERNAL SOLID MASONRY BUTTRESSES BRACE THIS BUILDING IN FRANCE AGAINST THE WIND.

Staying Warm

The earliest human settlements were centered in subtropical regions that had adequate food and water resources and arable land. As settlements spread to the more temperate regions, the problem of staying warm during the winter became critical. Caves offered limited protection, but as civilization grew, more successful ways of dealing with the cold were found.

The choice of the dwelling site was very important. The intention was to maximize the natural advantages of the site — such as terrain, geology, hydrology, vegetation, etc. — and minimize the impact of the cold.

The Anasazi Indians at Mesa Verde built their dwellings into rock cliffs. These niches faced south for the warming sun and gave sanctuary from the cold winds.

Balcony House
Mesa Verde, Colorado
13th Century

Hill Dwellings, Pakistan

In the mountains of Pakistan the people build their houses on steep, south-facing slopes to give shelter on the north and to capture the sun's warmth. This practice also leaves the entire river valley free for cultivation.

ANOTHER VERY EFFECTIVE WAY TO REDUCE
A DWELLING'S EXPOSURE TO THE COLD IS TO USE
BUILDING SHAPES THAT MAXIMIZE THE SPACE CONTAINED
WHILE MINIMIZING THE EXPOSED SURFACE AREA.

Sphere
VOLUME = 36 UNITS^3
SURFACE AREA = 52.7 UNITS^2
VOLUME/SURFACE AREA RATIO = .68

OVENBIRD NEST

Hemisphere
VOLUME = 36 UNITS^3
SURFACE AREA = 62.78 UNITS^2
VOLUME/SURFACE AREA RATIO = .57

INUIT IGLOO

Cube
VOLUME = 36 UNITS^3
SURFACE AREA = 65.4 UNITS^2
VOLUME/SURFACE AREA RATIO = .55

CANADIAN LOG CABIN

Rectangular Solid
VOLUME = 36 UNITS^3
SURFACE AREA = 96 UNITS^2
VOLUME/SURFACE AREA RATIO = .38

CONTEMPORARY
HAWAIIAN HOUSE

BY CLUSTERING MANY
DWELLING UNITS IN A
SINGLE MASS, THE
EXPOSED SURFACE
AREA CAN BE
SIGNIFICANTLY
REDUCED.

ACOMA PUEBLO
NEW MEXICO

SOME BEES AND WASPS USE
HEXAGONAL TUBES IN HIVE
BUILDING. THIS SHAPE ENCLOSES
A GOOD DEAL OF VOLUME AND
ALLOWS TIGHT PACKING OF THE
MODULES FOR MINIMUM EXPOSURE.

SECTION OF
HONEYBEE HIVE

A SIMPLE, EFFECTIVE, AND LOW-COST WAY IN WHICH TO REDUCE THE IMPACT OF THE COLD IS TO USE THE EARTH TO TEMPER THE HOUSE. SLIGHTLY BELOW THE FROST LINE SOIL WILL REMAIN AT ABOUT 50° F. YEAR-ROUND.

BANKED HOUSE CHESTER CO., PENNSYLVANIA
BY BUILDING INTO A SLOPE THE LOWER FLOOR IS PROTECTED BY EARTH ON THREE SIDES.

TEMPORARY MOUNTAIN SHELTER, PAKISTAN — EARTH AND ROCKS ARE PILED UP AROUND PART OF THE STRUCTURE.

ESKIMO EARTH-SHELTERED DWELLING, CANADA —
EARTH COVERS BOTH WALLS AND ROOF.

FARMHOUSE NORTHERN ICELAND — BUILT INTO HILLS WITH EARTH SHIELDING THE ROOF AND WALLS

LOG-END CAVE HOUSE, WEST CHAZY, NEW YORK — ONLY ONE WALL IS EXPOSED, WHILE EARTH PROTECTS THE REST OF THE HOUSE.

WHERE GEOLOGICAL CONDITIONS WERE FAVORABLE, MANY BUILDERS CHOSE TO COMPLETELY SHELTER THEMSELVES WITH THE LAND BY DIGGING INTO IT. THESE TROGLODYTE DWELLINGS BECAME VERY ELABORATE AND NOT AT ALL CAVE-LIKE.

SETENIL, SPAIN

SECTIONAL VIEW

EXISTING ROCK CREVICES WERE EXPANDED AND VARIED STRUCTURES AND FACADES ADDED.

CEREMONIAL KIVA MESA VERDE, COLORADO (1200)

KIVAS WERE CIRCULAR STONE STRUCTURES SUNKEN INTO THE GROUND, WITH A WOOD CEILING THAT SUPPORTED A LAYER OF EARTH. ORIGINALLY THESE WERE CEREMONIAL BUILDINGS, BUT LATER DWELLINGS TOOK THIS SHAPE ALSO.

TROGLODYTE DWELLINGS NORTHERN CHINA
THESE HOMES, CARVED INTO SOFT LOESS, LEFT THE SURFACE FREE FOR FARMING.

UNESCO HEADQUARTERS PARIS

WHILE THE FIRST STEP TAKEN TO INSURE STAYING WARM IS TO MINIMIZE THE DWELLING'S EXPOSURE TO THE COLD, THE SECOND IS TO MAXIMIZE THE STRUCTURE'S ABILITY TO GAIN AND HOLD HEAT FROM NATURAL SOURCES, PRIMARILY THE SUN. SITING, ORIENTATION, MATERIALS USED, ZONING OF SPACES, AND PLACEMENT OF OPENINGS ARE ALL MAJOR CONSIDERATIONS IN ACHIEVING EFFECTIVE SOLAR HEAT GAIN.

NORTH

PLAN OF PUEBLO BONITO, NEW MEXICO (A.D. 919)

THE PUEBLO INDIANS AT PUEBLO BONITO ORIENTED THEIR LIVING COMPLEX SO THAT IT TOOK MAXIMUM ADVANTAGE OF THE WINTER SUN FROM DAWN (1) TO DUSK (2) WHILE PROVIDING SHADE FROM THE HOT AFTERNOON SUN IN SUMMER (3).

EARTH BERM

LIVING AREA

PATIO   NORTH

JACOBS HOUSE WISCONSIN
FRANK LLOYD WRIGHT USED THE SAME ORIENTATION PRINCIPLES HERE IN 1943.

NORTH

ROMAN HOUSE (A.D. 50)

THIS PLAN OFFERED A PROTECTED SUNNY COURT PLUS A LARGE SOUTHERN EXPOSURE FOR THE MAIN LIVING SPACE

NORTH

PLAN OF QUEBEC HOUSE (1831)

NOTE THE PREDOMINANCE OF WINDOWS ON THE SOUTH SIDE FOR SOLAR HEAT GAIN.

STORAGE   BED-ROOM

KITCHEN

NORTH

SLEEPING + LIVING   LIVING

PLAN OF SWISS HOUSE

THE ZONING OF SPACES IN THIS HOUSE PUTS THE MAJOR LIVING AREAS ON THE SUNNY SOUTH SIDE WHILE STORAGE AND OTHER LESS USED SPACES ARE ON THE NORTH.

SOUTH DAKOTA FARMHOUSE
EARLY 20th CENTURY

THIS HOUSE IS ORIENTED SO THAT THE MAJOR LIVING SPACE HAS A WARM, PROTECTED SOUTHERN EXPOSURE. THE KITCHEN/WORK EL ON THE LEFT (WEST) SHADES MUCH OF THE SOUTH WALL FROM THE HOT AFTERNOON SUN IN THE SUMMER.

COMPASS TERMITE MOUND
AUSTRALIA

THESE TALL (UP TO 13 FEET) BLADE-LIKE MOUNDS ARE ORIENTED ON A PRECISE NORTH/SOUTH LINE. THE TERMITES SPEND THE MORNINGS ON THE EAST SIDE AND THEN MOVE TO THE WEST (WITH THE SUN) IN THE AFTERNOON.

WALL OF PUBLIC BATHS POMPEII (80 B.C.) THIS SOUTH-FACING GLAZED WALL ADDED A LARGE AMOUNT OF SOLAR HEAT TO THE BATHING SPACES INSIDE.

COLONIAL SALTBOX HOUSE
NEW HAMPSHIRE (1860's)

THE MAJORITY OF FIRST- AND SECOND-FLOOR WINDOWS FACED SOUTH FOR SOLAR HEAT GAIN WHILE MOST OF THE NORTH SIDE WAS ROOF TO OFFER PROTECTION FROM THE NORTH WINDS.

ENTRANCE (BY LADDER)

3

2

1

SECTION THROUGH ACOMA PUEBLO NEW MEXICO (A.D. 900) STORAGE SPACES (1) AND SLEEPING AREAS (2) TAKE UP LOWER AND NORTH-FACING PARTS OF BUILDING WITH THE MAIN LIVING AREA (3) BEING ABOVE AND FACING SOUTH.

THE DESIRE FOR SOLAR HEAT AND NATURAL
LIGHT PUT GREAT EMPHASIS ON THE
DESIGN AND USE
OF WINDOWS.

SUNLIGHT

SOUTH FACADE

ROMAN HELIOCAMINUS
OSTIA   (1ˢᵀ CENTURY)

THE GLAZED SOUTH WALL ADDED
INTENSE HEAT TO THE PUBLIC
BATHS WHILE ALSO KEEPING
IN THE WARM MOIST AIR.

NEW MEXICO (1816)
PIECES OF SELENITE (CRYSTAL-
LIZED GYPSUM) WERE USED
AS A GLAZING.

WINDOW   FRAME

PLAN OF STONE WINDOW FRAMES
MEDIEVAL ENGLAND

THE BEVELED SASH ADMITTED
A WIDER ANGLE OF SUNLIGHT
WITHOUT AN INCREASE IN
ACTUAL WINDOW SIZE.

GUARDA, PORTUGAL
THIS STRUCTURE'S BEVELED
SASH AND SILLS SERVE THE
SAME PURPOSE.

EARLY GREECE

PROJECTING SOLARIA ADDED
HEAT AND LIGHT TO HOMES.

TUCSON, ARIZONA
THIS CONTEMPORARY HOUSE USES
A SUNSPACE FOR DIRECT SOLAR GAIN.

32

SUNLIGHT

IN HOT, ARID AREAS, DENSE HEAT-ABSORBING MATERIALS CAN MODERATE THE LARGE DAILY TEMPERATURE FLUCTUATIONS BY ABSORBING HEAT DURING THE DAY AND SLOWLY RELEASING IT AT NIGHT.

THERMAL MASS
AS A MODERATOR OF TEMPERATURE SWINGS

OUTSIDE TEMP. ——
INSIDE TEMP. – – –

C

A   B

TIME OF DAY: 6 A.M.   NOON   6 P.M.   12 P.M.   6 A.M.

THE DEGREE OF TEMPERATURE VARIATION OUTSIDE (A) IS GREATLY REDUCED INSIDE (B) BECAUSE THE PEAK EFFECT OF THE DAY'S HEAT IS DELAYED BY THE THERMAL MASS TO A TIME WHEN IT IS COUNTERBALANCED BY THE COOL OF THE NIGHT. THUS THE BUILDING HELPS COOL ITSELF DURING THE DAY AND HEAT ITSELF AT NIGHT. THIS TIME DELAY IN THERMAL EFFECTS IS CALLED THE THERMAL LAG.

MATERIALS TRADITIONALLY USED IN THIS WAY INCLUDE MUD, ADOBE, STONE, BRICK, TILE, AND CONCRETE.

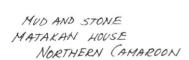

MUD AND STONE
MATAKAN HOUSE
NORTHERN CAMAROON

ADOBE PUEBLO
NEW MEXICO

SOME OTHER METHODS OF STORING HEAT IN THERMAL MASS MATERIALS:

BRICK THERMAL WALL GREENHOUSE (1700's)

"DRUMWALL" ALBUQUERQUE, NEW MEXICO (WATER-FILLED DRUMS BEHIND GLASS) (1975)

A THICK MASONRY WALL DIRECTLY BEHIND SOUTH-FACING GLASS CAN STORE A GREAT DEAL OF HEAT, AND AIR CAN FLOW BETWEEN THE WALL AND GLASS TO HELP DISTRIBUTE THAT HEAT.

MORSE WALL (1881)

TROMBE WALL (OR TROMWALL) (1981)

WATER CAN STORE MORE HEAT THAN OTHER MATERIALS, BUT SPECIAL CHEMICALS DESIGNED TO CHANGE PHASE (FROM SOLID TO LIQUID) AT CERTAIN TEMPERATURES CAN DO EVEN BETTER.

WATER COLUMNS CONCORD, NEW HAMPSHIRE (1980)

PHASE-CHANGE CEILING PANELS IN EXPERIMENTAL HOUSE, MASSACHUSETTS (1975)

MANY EARLY
DWELLINGS WERE
PROTECTED BY A
BLANKET OF EARTH
TO ACT AS AN
INSULATOR.

EARLY ARMENIAN DWELLING
THIS EARTH-SHELTERED STRUCTURE
ACCOMMODATED BOTH HUMANS (ON
THE RIGHT) AND ANIMALS.

MANDAN EARTH LODGE
UPPER MISSOURI VALLEY

INUIT IGLOO, CANADA
BOTH ICE AND SNOW ACT
AS INSULATORS AGAINST THE
SUB-ZERO TEMPERATURES
AND HARSH WINDS.

FARMHOUSE, HOKKAIDO,
JAPAN

EVEN WITH A STEEP
PITCH (FOR STRUCTURAL
SUPPORT) THE TEXTURE
OF THE WOOD ROOF HELPS
RETAIN AN INSULATING
BLANKET OF SNOW.

LOG CABIN
QUEBEC
A LAYER OF EARTH ON
THE CEILING ACTS AS INSU-
LATION.

KIRGHIZIAN YURT

INSULATION

IN COLD WEATHER, ADDITIONAL LAYERS OF HEAVY FELT BLANKETS, OR MUNDAHS, WERE PLACED ON THE YURT FOR EXTRA INSULATION.

IN SOME INSTANCES HAY BALES WERE USED AS STRUCTURAL ELEMENTS, AND THEY ALSO PROVIDED GOOD INSULATION.

HAY BALE BARN NEBRASKA (1910)

NEW HAMPSHIRE HOUSE (1850)

HAY BALES WERE (AND STILL ARE) USED AS INSU-LATION AROUND HOUSE FOUNDATIONS IN NEW ENGLAND. IN THE MIDWEST, MANURE IS SOMETIMES USED FOR THIS PURPOSE.

WASPS MAKE PAPER WITH WHICH THEY BUILD THEIR NESTS. THE THIN SHELL WITH MANY AIR POCKETS INSULATES AS WELL AS 16 INCHES OF BRICK.

WALL OF PAPER WASP NEST

EARLY HOME BUILDERS FILLED THE CAVITY BETWEEN INNER AND OUTER WALLS WITH PAPER OR STRAW FOR INSULATION. BUILDERS TODAY USE FIBERGLASS, CELLULOSE, FOAMS, AND OTHER MATERIALS.

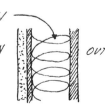

STOPPING HEAT LOSS CAUSED BY THE INFILTRATION OF COLD AIR

CHINKING OF MUD PLUS SKINS HUNG ON THE INSIDE WALL STOPPED UP THE AIR LEAKS BETWEEN LOGS.

LOG CABIN WALL
U.S. (1800's)

PLASTER ON STONE WALLS SEALED GAPS.

PENNSYLVANIA HOUSE (1800)

SIMPLE EXTERIOR SOLID SHUTTERS

NEW YORK (1706)

BRIEFLY HEATING AN IGLOO AFTER CONSTRUCTION FORMS AN ICE LAYER INSIDE THAT SEALS CRACKS. SKINS HUNG INSIDE HELP INSULATE, TOO.
INUIT IGLOO, CANADA

MANY IGLOOS HAVE THE ENTRANCE BELOW THE LIVING LEVEL SO THAT THE WARM AIR (WHICH RISES) DOES NOT ESCAPE.

EARLY FARMHOUSES IN THE MIDWEST AND EASTERN U.S. HAD A "DOUBLE ENTRY" - THE ATTACHED SPACE ACTED AS A BUFFER TO PREVENT DIRECT LOSS OF HEAT.

REVOLVING DOORS REDUCE HEAT LOSS BY ELIMINATING PATHS FOR DIRECT AIR FLOW BETWEEN INSIDE AND OUTSIDE.

EXTERIOR PANEL
SHUTTERS, VIRGINIA
(1700's)

FUTURASAN SHRINE, NIKKO, JAPAN
THE EXTERIOR SHUTTERS (A) HERE ARE
SOLID FOR INSULATION WHILE THE
INTERIOR ONES (B) ARE TRANSLUCENT
TO ADMIT NATURAL LIGHT. METAL
BRACKETS FROM THE CEILING HOLD
THEM OPEN.

SLIDING INDIAN SHUTTERS
YORK, MAINE (1800)

BIFOLD INTERIOR SHUTTERS
PHILADELPHIA (1850)
THESE FOLD BACK NEATLY INTO THE
WALL.

ICEHOUSE WINDOW
SHAKER VILLAGE,
HANCOCK, MASSACHUSETTS
EARLY USE OF MULTIPLE GLAZING
TO CUT DOWN HEAT FLOW

CONTEMPORARY HOUSE
VERMONT
PANELS ARE LOWERED
OVER WINDOWS AT
NIGHT TO REDUCE HEAT
LOSS.

IN REVIEW, TO BEST RETAIN HEAT AND PROTECT AGAINST COLD, BUILDERS MUST:

1) MINIMIZE THE STRUCTURE'S EXPOSURE TO THE COLD;
2) MINIMIZE THE HEAT LOSS FROM THE STRUCTURE BY USING VARIOUS INSULATING TECHNIQUES;
3) MAXIMIZE THE NATURAL HEAT GAINS FROM SUN AND EARTH.

AFTER THESE GUIDELINES HAVE BEEN FOLLOWED THERE MAY STILL BE A NEED FOR ADDITIONAL HEATING. THIS CAN BE SUPPLIED BY A VARIETY OF MEANS.

SOME ANTS HEAT THEIR COLONY BY TAKING TURNS SITTING OUT IN THE SUN SOAKING UP ITS RADIANT HEAT AND THEN GOING BACK INSIDE TO ACT AS LIVING PORTABLE HEATERS. WASPS AND BEES CAN HEAT THEIR HIVES WITH THE INCREASED BODY HEAT GENERATED THROUGH THE MUSCULAR EXERTION OF FLEXING THEIR ABDOMENS OR FLAPPING THEIR WINGS.

THE EARLY HUMAN SHELTERS RELIED PRIMARILY ON TWO HEAT SOURCES:

1) FIRE
2) BODY HEAT FROM PEOPLE AND ANIMALS

EUROPEAN LONGHOUSE (1100)
THE ANIMALS IN THE BYRE HELPED TO HEAT THIS PRIMITIVE SHELTER.

ONANDAGA LONGHOUSE
NORTH AMERICA, 15th CENTURY

THE FIRES AND THE NUMEROUS OCCUPANTS COMBINED TO HEAT THESE LARGE (UP TO 125 FEET IN LENGTH) COMMUNAL DWELLINGS.

HEAT PRODUCTION OF AVERAGE PERSON:

SEATED	– 110 WATTS *
LIGHT WORK	– 170 WATTS
HEAVY WORK	– 440 WATTS

* FOR COMPARISON, A 100-WATT INCANDESCENT LIGHT PRODUCES APPROXIMATELY 96 WATTS OF HEAT.

THE BRUSH TURKEY BUILDS ITS BROODING MOUND BY GATHERING A LARGE PILE OF PLANT MATERIAL, PLACING THE EGGS ON TOP, AND COVERING THEM WITH SAND. THE FERMENTATION OF THE PLANTS GENERATES THE HEAT TO INCUBATE THE EGGS.

COMPOST — EGGS — SAND

BRUSH TURKEY BROODING MOUND

A SINGLE WHALE OIL LAMP IN AN IGLOO CAN MAINTAIN A COMFORTABLE TEMPERATURE.

INUIT IGLOO, CANADA

SMOKE HOLE

EARLY INDIAN DWELLINGS IN THE SOUTHWESTERN U.S. RELIED UPON AN OPEN FIREPIT FOR HEAT WITH A SMOKE HOLE IN THE EARTH ROOF.

INDIAN DWELLING, AMERICAN SOUTHWEST (A.D. 500)

EARLY SETTLERS IN JAMESTOWN BUILT HUTS THAT HAD WALLS OF WATTLE (STICKS WITH INTERWOVEN TWIGS) AND DAUB (MUD), AND ROOFS OF THATCH. THE HOUSES HAD OPEN HEARTHS AND NO CHIMNEYS EXCEPT FOR THE SHORT OUTLET AT THE ROOF.

JAMESTOWN, VIRGINIA (CA. 1608)

THROUGHOUT HISTORY THE MOST COMMON
FUEL USED FOR SPACE HEATING HAS
BEEN WOOD.

JAPANESE RO

FOR CENTURIES IN JAPAN
WOOD HAS BEEN PROCESSED INTO
CHARCOAL, WHICH IS THEN BURNED
IN HEARTHS SET INTO THE FLOOR (ROS)

HIBACHI

OR IN PORTABLE HIBACHIS. CHARCOAL COMBUSTION
YIELDS VERY LITTLE SMOKE, SO
CHIMNEYS WERE NOT BUILT.

ENGLISH HEARTH
16th CENTURY
THE BIG HEARTH HAD
SPACE ENOUGH FOR A
NICE WARM WORK SPACE
AND A WINDOW.

DUTCH HEARTH, 17th CENTURY

THE WIDE, DEEP HEARTH WITH ITS
CANTILEVERED HOOD BROUGHT THE
FIRE'S WARMTH RIGHT OUT INTO
THE ROOM.

QUAKER FIREPLACES
19th CENTURY

THE CORNER
FIREPLACE
RADIATES HEAT
WELL THROUGHOUT THE ROOM, AND
THIS BACK-TO-BACK SCHEME
ALLOWS TWO FIREPLACES TO SHARE
ONE CHIMNEY, THEREBY REDUCING
THE AMOUNT OF CONSTRUCTION
THAT IS REQUIRED.

HOODED FIREPLACE WITH
A BRICK HEARTH
NEW MEXICO (19th CENTURY)

KOREAN K'ANG

IN THIS HEATING SYSTEM THE HOT GASES FROM THE FIRE WEAVE UNDER THE DWELLING FLOOR BEFORE GOING OUT THE CHIMNEY. THE ENTIRE FLOOR THEN ACTS AS A RADIANT HEATER. THE ROMANS USED A SIMILAR SYSTEM BUT WERE ABLE TO HEAT ALL SIX SURFACES SURROUNDING THE SPACE.

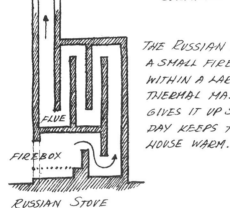

RUSSIAN STOVE

THE RUSSIAN MASONRY STOVE CONSISTS OF A SMALL FIREBOX AND A WINDING FLUE WITHIN A LARGE MASONRY MASS. THIS THERMAL MASS STORES THE HEAT AND GIVES IT UP SLOWLY. ONE SMALL FIRE PER DAY KEEPS THE HOUSE WARM.

KACHELOFEN

THE AUSTRIAN KACHELOFEN USES THERMAL MASS PRINCIPLES LIKE THE RUSSIAN STOVE AND IS USUALLY TILED. THE LOADING DOOR IS OFTEN BEHIND THE WALL IN AN ADJACENT ROOM OR HALLWAY.

IN THIS HOUSE IN BREWSTER, MASSACHUSETTS THE CHIMNEY IS CENTRALLY LOCATED SO IT CAN GIVE ITS HEAT TO THE INTERIOR SPACES RATHER THAN TO THE OUTDOORS.

THE INVENTION OF THE WOODSTOVE ALLOWED THE HEAT SOURCE TO BE MOVED OUT INTO THE ROOM. SUCH A CENTRAL LOCATION GAVE BALANCED RADIATION AND CONVECTION THROUGHOUT WHILE THE LONG RUN OF STOVEPIPE TO THE CHIMNEY SERVED AS AN ADDITIONAL RADIATOR OF HEAT THAT WAS PREVIOUSLY LOST UP THE CHIMNEY.

PLAN OF QUEBEC HOUSE

NEW ENGLAND FARMHOUSE

NATURAL CONVECTIVE CURRENTS RATHER THAN FANS WERE THE DRIVING FORCES BEHIND THE DISTRIBUTION OF THE WOODSTOVE'S HEAT. GRATES WERE USUALLY PLACED IN THE CEILING ABOVE THE STOVE TO ALLOW WARM AIR TO RISE TO THE SECOND FLOOR.

POTBELLY STOVE

THE SOMEWHAT SPHERICAL SHAPE OF THE OLD POTBELLY STOVE MADE IT A VERY EFFECTIVE RADIATOR.

IN ORDER TO YIELD AS MUCH HEAT AS POSSIBLE, MANY WOODSTOVE DESIGNS INCORPORATED LARGE HEAT EXCHANGERS TO EXTRACT HEAT FROM THE HOT FLUE PIPES.

VERMONT SOAPSTONE STOVE

BECAUSE OF THEIR GREAT THERMAL MASS, SOAPSTONE STOVES HEAT UP AND COOL DOWN SLOWLY, WHICH RESULTS IN A RELATIVELY EVEN HEAT OVER A LONG PERIOD.

ANOTHER METHOD OF EFFECTIVELY DISTRIBUTING
HEAT IS TO TRANSPORT THE HEAT
SOURCE TO WHERE IT
IS NEEDED.

JAPANESE PORTABLE
KEROSENE HEATER
(USED NOW)

PORTABLE CHARCOAL BRAZIER
USED IN OLYNTHUS, GREECE
(400 B.C.)

CONTEMPORARY METHODS
OF DISTRIBUTING HEAT
WITH FANS AND PUMPS
HAVE PERMITTED HOUSES
TO BECOME SPREAD OUT
AND FRAGMENTED. THIS
RESULTS IN A SPATIAL
CONFIGURATION THAT IS MUCH
LESS EFFICIENT TO HEAT THAN THE OLD
CENTRALIZED PLAN (SEE HOUSE
PLAN TO THE LEFT).

ONE OF THE MOST RAPIDLY DEVEL-
OPING HEATING TECHNOLOGIES IS
SOLAR. A BASIC ACTIVE SOLAR
SYSTEM CONSISTS OF A COLLECTOR,
A DISTRIBUTION NETWORK, AND
A HEAT STORAGE RESERVOIR.
THE COLLECTOR ABSORBS THE SUN'S HEAT AND
TRANSFERS IT TO A FLUID (USUALLY AIR
OR WATER). THE HEAT IS THEN
EITHER STORED OR USED IMMEDI-
ATELY TO HEAT THE HOUSE OR
THE DOMESTIC WATER.

MOST CONTEMPORARY SOLAR
HOMES COMBINE ACTIVE SYSTEMS
(THOSE NEEDING ENERGY INPUT)
AND PASSIVE SYSTEMS SUCH AS
ATTACHED GREENHOUSES, EXTRA
SOUTH GLAZING, THERMAL MASS,
AND MANY MORE.

CONTEMPORARY SOLAR HOUSE

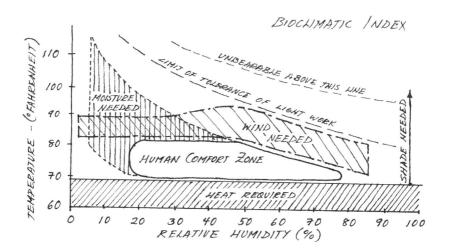

BIOCLIMATIC INDEX

THE ABOVE BIOCLIMATIC INDEX OUTLINES THE RELATIONSHIP BETWEEN TEMPERATURE, HUMIDITY, AND HUMAN COMFORT. WHEN CONDITIONS ARE ABOVE THE HUMAN COMFORT ZONE IT IS NECESSARY TO INTRODUCE A COOLING INFLUENCE SUCH AS SHADING, VENTILATION, OR ADDED MOISTURE.

THIS INFORMATION HAS MANY IMPORTANT HOUSING DESIGN IMPLICATIONS IN AREAS WHERE COOLING IS REQUIRED. THESE GUIDELINES VARY WITH THE CLIMATE:

A) HOT-ARID CLIMATE: 1) TAKE ADVANTAGE OF THE BROAD DAILY TEMPERATURE VARIATION BY USING MATERIALS THAT ABSORB THE DAY'S HEAT FOR RERADIATION AT NIGHT AND BY TRAPPING AND HOLDING COOL NIGHT AIR, 2) GIVE PLENTY OF SHADING, AND 3) MINIMIZE DAYTIME VENTILATION

B) HOT-HUMID CLIMATE: 1) SITE, ORIENT, AND CONSTRUCT THE HOUSE TO TAKE MAXIMUM ADVANTAGE OF NATURAL VENTILATION, 2) USE POROUS NON-HEAT-ABSORBING MATERIALS, AND 3) SUPPLY ADEQUATE SHADING.

THE WAYS IN WHICH THE HUMAN BODY DISSIPATES HEAT:

RADIATION	–	44 %
CONVECTION	–	32 %
EVAPORATION	–	21 %
CONDUCTION	–	3 %

SUMMER

WINTER

BEYOND THE ADVANTAGES PREVIOUSLY
MENTIONED, THE CLIFFS AT MESA VERDE,
COLORADO OFFERED SHADE FROM THE HOT
SUMMER SUN BUT ADMITTED THE SUN'S
NEEDED WARMTH IN WINTER.

CLIFF DWELLINGS
MESA VERDE, COLORADO
(1200)

HERE, THE SHADE OFFERED
BY TREES IS AUGMENTED BY A
SUSPENDED, GRASS-COVERED NET
TO SHIELD THE HAMMOCK.

COLOMBIA

NEW MEXICO

LOCATING DWELLINGS BY RIVERS
OFFERS FRESH WATER AND
TREES FOR SHADE, AND THE
VALLEY TRAPS THE HEAVIER
COOL AIR.

IN AREAS WHERE
WIND IS THE PRIMARY COOLING
AGENT, IT MAY BE ADVANTAGEOUS
TO PUT THE HOUSE ON AN EXPOSED HILL.

WINDS

IN ADDITION TO SUPPLYING
AN ALL-IMPORTANT
SANCTUARY FROM
CLOUDS OF MOSQUITOES,
THESE HOUSES, PLACED IN
TREES OUT IN THE
WATER, WERE COOL
RETREATS FROM THE
TROPICAL HEAT.

ORINOCO DELTA, VENEZUELA (1600)

Shading

Early man, like the apes, relied chiefly upon the plants around him to create shade.

In this case, a lean-to of branches and leaves protects the hammock occupant from rain and sun.

PRIMITIVE LEAN-TO

The Navaho summer shelter, or ramada, has a simple pole frame and a roof of poles and brush. It gives shade while letting the cool breezes flow through.

The Yokut Indians of Southern California built pole and brush shade roofs over whole groups of huts.

YOKUT TULE LODGE, CALIFORNIA

In many warm climates shelter takes the form of an umbrella to protect from the rain and to give shade from the sun.

SENUFO OUTDOOR KITCHEN, IVORY COAST

IN ASIA THE TENT HAS EVOLVED OVER THOUSANDS OF YEARS INTO A VERY HIGHLY DEVELOPED AND SOMETIMES ELABORATE SHELTER FROM SUN AND RAIN.

CHINESE MILITARY PAVILION

SUNLIGHT

SOME BUILDINGS HAVE PROJECTING UPPER STORIES THAT, IN ADDITION TO ADDING MORE SPACE, CREATE A COVERED WALK BELOW AND SHADE MUCH OF THE LOWER RECESSED WALL.

SECTION OF CASA ISOLANI

CASA ISOLANI, BOLOGNA, ITALY (1200)

ANOTHER WAY TO KEEP THE SUN FROM OVERHEATING A BUILDING IS TO CREATE A HIGHLY TEXTURED FACADE SO THAT THE PROTRUSIONS ACTUALLY SHADE THE REST OF THE WALL.

MOUSGOUM HOMESTEAD NORTHERN CAMEROON

DOGON HOUSE SANGA, MALI

TRELLIS, OR PERGOLA, OVER DOORWAY

TRANI HOUSE
APULIA, ITALY

WIRE LATTICE USED AS A TRELLIS FOR VINES SHADING COURT

SHADED COURT, GRANADA, SPAIN

↑ NORTH

HOUSE

TREES

AN OLD NEW ENGLAND TRADITION IS TO PLANT HUSBAND AND WIFE TREES TO GIVE SUMMER SHADE TO THE HOUSE'S SOUTH SIDE WHEN IT IS MOST VULNERABLE IN THE MORNING AND EVENING.

FARMHOUSE
NEW HAMPSHIRE

IN MANY AREAS ELABORATE IRON GRILLWORK IS USED AS A LATTICE FOR VINES TO SHADE THE HOUSE.

DOUBLE-TRELLISED HOUSE IN NEW ORLEANS, LOUISIANA

IN MOST WARM CLIMATES A GREAT DEAL OF THE ACTIVITY TAKES PLACE OUTSIDE. THE NEED TO SUPPLY SHADE IN OUTDOOR PUBLIC PLACES SPAWNED A WIDE VARIETY OF SHADES AND SUNSCREENS.

CANVAS AWNINGS, OR TOLDOS, UNFURLED BETWEEN BUILDINGS   SEVILLE, SPAIN

RIGID FRAMES ROOFED WITH SPACED POLES ALSO SHADE STREETS AND WALK- WAYS EFFECTIVELY.

COVERED STREET
TAOS, NEW MEXICO

SIMPLE POLE-SUPPORTED AWNING

MYKONOS, GREECE

WOOD LATTICE SUNSCREEN

AFRICAN BAZAAR

COVERED PORCHES HAVE BEEN USED FOR THOUSANDS OF YEARS AS A SHADY SANCTUARY FROM THE HOT SUN.

DOUBLE HOUSE
SAN ANTONIO, TEXAS

DORDOGNE, FRANCE

ARCADES CAN PROVIDE BOTH SHADE AND PROTECTION FROM RAIN AND SNOW.

PORCH ROOFS SUPPLY SHADE AND CAN ALSO BE USED AS ADDITIONAL LIVING OR SLEEPING AREAS.

SANTA FE,
NEW MEXICO

SOME HOUSES HAVE PORCHES THAT WRAP ALMOST ENTIRELY AROUND THEM.

HACIENDA, VENEZUELA

THE RAISED BALCONY, OR LOGGIA, IS A VERY COMMON SIGHT IN WARM CLIMATES. THESE STRUCTURES CREATE RELATIVELY PRIVATE LIVING SPACES THAT ARE EXPOSED TO THE COOLING BREEZES. THEY ALSO CAN SHADE THE LOWER FLOOR.

LOGGIA, PEDRAZA, SPAIN

PROJECTING BALCONY
AFGHANISTAN

THIS LOGGIA IS PARTLY WINDOWED, PARTLY OPEN, AND PARTLY FITTED WITH LOUVERED SHUTTERS.

MYKONOS, GREECE

THIS LOGGIA FACES A SERENE, SHADED COURT AND ALSO SHELTERS THE PORCH BELOW, WHICH ACTS AS THE ENTRANCE.

CHARLESTON,
SOUTH CAROLINA

SHADING THE OPENINGS

In a warm climate it is important to design openings that admit the cooling winds but not the heat of the sun. One way to do this is to recess the window or door so that the depth of the wall shades much of the opening.

PUEBLO WINDOW NEW MEXICO

DOORWAY, AFGHANISTAN

Shading devices such as roofs, shutters, awnings, lattices, and louvers are also effective.

AFGHAN WINDOW MAYDAN VALLEY

Horizontally hinged shutters double as shades. KAVALLA, GREECE

This window combines shutters, lattice screens, and louvers for good ventilation and plenty of privacy.

JEDDAH, SAUDI ARABIA

For centuries louvered shutters have been used as a means of shutting out the hot sun but allowing the cooling breezes to flow through.

Doorway with Louvered Shutter, Fossacesia, Italy

SUNLIGHT

WIND

Sectional View

Contemporary louvered awning shutter, Florida

Adjustable, vertical-axis louvers, or vanes, are also very effective shading devices.

Contemporary House Rio de Janeiro

Other shades:

Exterior, Metal Roll Shade Luxembourg

Projecting Sunscreen Nara, Japan

PLACING THE SCREENS
OR LOUVERED SHUTTERS
AWAY FROM THE WINDOWS
CAUSES LESS INTER-
FERENCE WITH THE AIR
FLOW THROUGH
THE HOUSE.

CONTEMPORARY HOUSE
SAN ANTONIO, TEXAS

CONTEMPORARY HOUSE
WITH PULLEY-OPERATED
SHUTTER/SHADE
PANELS

SANIBEL ISLAND,
FLORIDA

PROPERLY DESIGNED OVERHANGS
CAN OFFER SHADE FROM
THE HIGH SUMMER SUN (1)
IN TEMPERATE AREAS
AND ADMIT THE
LOW WINTER SUN (2).

SUNLIGHT

THE ROOF OF THIS AFRICAN
HOUSE SHADES THE WINDOW,
AND THE GRASS PATCH
PREVENTS SUNLIGHT
FROM BEING REFLECTED
INSIDE.

CONTEMPORARY OVERHANG
LOS ANGELES, CALIFORNIA

VENTILATION

OPEN AND ELEVATED HOUSES ARE
BUILT IN HOT, HUMID AREAS
PARTLY BECAUSE THEY TAKE
EXCELLENT ADVANTAGE OF
THE COOLING BREEZES.

RAISED PLATFORM
SEMINOLE BUILDING,
FLORIDA

TREE HOUSE

NEW GUINEA

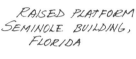

THE OPEN PLANNING OF VILLAGES IS ALSO
ESSENTIAL FOR GOOD AIR FLOW.

AIR MOVEMENT THROUGH A
BARI VILLAGE, SUDAN

OPEN SAMOAN HUT

NOTE THE OPEN
SECOND FLOOR IN THIS TWO-
THOUSAND-YEAR-OLD CLAY
MODEL OF A MINOAN
HOUSE.

OPEN PORCH, NEW ORLEANS (1800's)

IN THE GREEK
VILLAGE OF VERRIA HOMES
FACING THE SAME STREET HAD
ROOFS OF DIFFERENT HEIGHTS
FOR ENOUGH SEPARATION TO
ENSURE GOOD AIR FLOW.

VERRIA,
EARLY GREECE

FLAT TILES CAN BE ARRANGED IN
SIMPLE PATTERNS TO CREATE GRILLES
THAT ADMIT AIR BUT
NOT SUNLIGHT.

KSAR-EL-BARKA,
MAURITANIA

LATTICE WALLS OF
REEDS AND POLES ARE
USED IN MANY PARTS OF
THE WORLD TO PERMIT
VENTILATION.

SOUTHERN TANZANIA

THE OPEN PLAN OF JAPANESE
HOUSES ALLOWS EXCELLENT VENTILATION. EVEN WITH THE
SLIDING FUSUMAS CLOSED, THE LOUVERED TRANSOM ABOVE
LETS AIR FLOW
THROUGH.

EXPOSITION HOUSE, MUSEUM OF MODERN ART, NEW YORK (1954)

ONE OF THE MOST WIDELY EMPLOYED DEVICES THAT GIVES SHADE AND ALSO ALLOWS VENTILATION IS THE LOUVERED SHUTTER.

MULTIPLE SHUTTER, MACAO

PORTISOL SHUTTER DUBROVNIK, YUGOSLAVIA

LEVER-OPERATED LOUVER PANEL TO OPEN OR CLOSE TRANSOM VENT

SHAKER DOOR HANCOCK, MASSACHUSETTS (1830)

IN ADDITION TO BEING SHADED BY THE LOGGIA ROOF, THIS DOORWAY HAS LOUVERED SHUTTERS AND A GLASS TRANSOM VENT FOR GOOD AIR FLOW.

FAURIE HOUSE, NEW ORLEANS (EARLY 1800's)

THE HIGHLY DECORATIVE
OPENINGS IN THIS SMITHY
INSURE GOOD
THROUGH-VENTILATION.

BIDA,
CENTRAL NIGERIA

TRADITIONAL
JAPANESE HOUSES
ARE EQUIPPED WITH
BAMBOO CURTAINS THAT
SCREEN THE SUNLIGHT BUT
LET AIR PASS THROUGH.

NUMAZU, JAPAN

STONE VENTILATION GRILLE
GUANAJUATO, MEXICO

DOOR WITH GRILLE FOR
LIGHT AND AIR
VERACRUZ, MEXICO

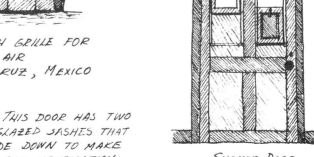

THIS DOOR HAS TWO
SMALL, GLAZED SASHES THAT
CAN SLIDE DOWN TO MAKE
OPENINGS FOR VENTILATION.

SHAKER DOOR
CANTERBURY, NEW HAMPSHIRE (1831)

INDUCED VENTILATION

THE NATURAL TENDENCY OF WARMER AIR TO RISE CAN BE USED AS THE DRIVING FORCE TO VENTILATE BUILDINGS. THE VENTING OF WARM AIR AT THE TOP WILL DRAW COOLER AIR IN AT THE BOTTOM.

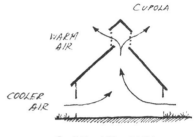

BARN AIR FLOW

CUPOLA ON A NEW HAMPSHIRE BARN

OPEN VENT

AMERICAN TOP HAT BARN

SECTION THROUGH CEREMONIAL UNDERGROUND KIVA

MESA VERDE, COLORADO

WARM AIR RISING OUT DRAWS OUTSIDE AIR THROUGH AN UNDERGROUND CHANNEL WHERE IT IS COOLED BEFORE IT ENTERS THE KIVA.

60

FOR MILLIONS OF YEARS, TERMITE COLONIES HAVE USED THERMAL CURRENTS, OR THERMOSIPHONING, TO DRIVE THEIR COOLING AND AIR PURIFICATION SYSTEMS.

AIR HEATED BY THE COLONY RISES TO THE TOP (1) AND THEN FLOWS INTO THE TRANSPIRATION TUBES (2), WHICH ACT LIKE COOLING FINS. AS THE AIR IS COOLED, IT SINKS TO THE BOTTOM OF THE COLONY (3), AND THE CYCLE CONTINUES. FRESH AIR IS ALSO ABSORBED THROUGH THE THIN WALLS OF THE TUBES.

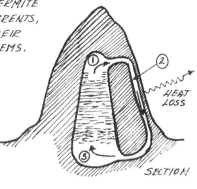

TERMITE MOUND

FOR CENTURIES IN THE MIDDLE EAST, BUILDERS HAVE USED A FORM OF COOLING TOWER IN HOMES. SUNLIGHT HEATS UP THE TALL TOWER, AND AS THE WARM AIR INSIDE RISES, IT PULLS COOL AIR IN BEHIND. SOMETIMES THIS AIR IS DRAWN OVER WATER FOR ADDITIONAL COOLING BY EVAPORATION.

IN THIS CONTEMPORARY SOLAR HOUSE, THE HEAT GENERATED BY SUNLIGHT IN THE GREENHOUSE CAUSES THE AIR TO RISE AND ESCAPE, AND AS IT DOES IT PULLS COOL AIR INTO THE LIVING AREAS.

CHANNELING THE WIND

DEVICES THAT COOL HOUSES BY DIRECTING THE WIND INSIDE HAVE BEEN USED FOR CENTURIES.

EGYPTIAN HOUSE WITH WIND SCOOPS
MIDDLE KINGDOM

PERUVIAN WIND SCOOP
(PRE – A.D. 700)

WIND SCOOP WITH TRAP DOOR
WEST PAKISTAN
(USED SINCE 1500's)

ROOFSCAPE
WITH WIND SCOOPS

SIND DISTRICT,
WEST PAKISTAN

WIND SCOOPS
ON ROOFTOPS

HERAT, AFGHANISTAN

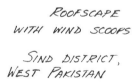

Thermal Mass

As the graph on page 33 shows, the proper use of heat-absorbing, or thermal mass, materials in hot, arid climates can heat a house during the night and cool it during the day. The earth is such a large mass that its temperature stays relatively constant year-round and can help warm a house in the winter and cool it in the summer.

PARTIAL PLAN OF ROMAN SUMMER CAVE

Other solid materials provide thermal mass:

BADAKSHAN DOMED, MUD HOUSE, AFGHANISTAN

MUD AND STONE WALLS

MATAKAM HOUSE CAMEROON

MUD AND STONE DOGON CLIFF DWELLINGS, MALI

STONE CLIFF DWELLINGS MESA VERDE, COLORADO

(1200)

THIS HOUSE CONSISTS OF
FIVE HUTS WITH THICK
ADOBE WALLS GROUPED
TO FORM A CENTRAL
COURT, WHICH IS
SHADED BY A
TRELLIS.

MESAKIN QUISAR CLUSTER DWELLING
SUDAN

THE GROUPING OF MANY DWELLINGS IN
A SINGLE, SOLID STRUCTURE PROVIDES A
LARGE THERMAL MASS AND ALSO
LEAVES A MINIMUM OF
SURFACE EXPOSED TO
THE HEAT.

DAMMUSO HOUSE
PANTELLERIA, ITALY

ADOBE PUEBLO
TAOS, NEW MEXICO

VAULTED HOUSES
GREECE

ROOF POND COOLING

DAY   INSULATION

HEAT TO
WATER

NIGHT

HEAT RADIATED
FROM WATER

THIS CONTEMPORARY COOLING SYSTEM USES A POND OF WATER
AS A HEAT SINK ON THE ROOF. INSULATED FROM THE SUN
DURING THE DAY, THE POND ABSORBS HEAT FROM THE HOUSE.
UNCOVERED AT NIGHT, IT CAN LOSE ITS HEAT TO THE SKY.

USING COURTYARDS
TO TRAP COOL AIR

THE TENDENCY OF
COOLER AIR TO SINK
PERMITS AN ENCLOSED COURT
TO EFFECTIVELY TRAP THE COOL
NIGHT AIR IN HOT, ARID AREAS.

COURT OF SUBTERRANEAN
DWELLING, TUNISIA

ASHANTI HOUSE, GHANA

THIS AFRICAN HOUSE
HAS AN ENCLOSED COURTYARD,
OR "GYAASE," TO GIVE SHADE
AND PRIVACY AND TO HOLD
COOL AIR.

IN MANY AREAS, A NUMBER
OF DWELLINGS ARE BUILT AROUND
A CENTRAL COURT, WHICH BECOMES
A SANCTUARY FROM THE HEAT.

EL OUED,
ALGERIA

TREE IN ENCLOSED
COURTYARD
VENEZUELA

THE COURTYARD IS
KEPT MUCH COOLER IF
IT IS FULLY SHADED
BY EITHER THE SURROUNDING
BUILDINGS (SEE ABOVE), BY
VINES (SEE PAGE 49), OR
BY TREES.

WATER WILL EVAPORATE AS IT ABSORBS HEAT FROM THE SURROUNDING AIR. THIS PROCESS, WHICH RESULTS IN THE AIR BEING COOLED, CAN BE USED TO HELP COOL HOUSES IN ARID CLIMATES.

A WATER-SOAKED CLOTH IN THE WINDOW COOLS THE INCOMING AIR.
INDIA

DINING PAVILIONS BUILT OVER WATER
CHINA

WIND

CUPOLA VENT

WARM AIR OUT

FOUNTAIN

YAZD, IRAN (1400)

IN IRAN SOME BUILDINGS HAVE TOWERS TO CATCH THE WIND AND DIRECT IT INSIDE, WHERE IT IS COOLED AS IT PASSES BY A FOUNTAIN OR POOL. THE WIND ALSO HELPS TO DRAW THE WARM AIR OUT AT THE CUPOLA (SEE PAGE 60).

A FOUNTAIN OR POOL IN A COURTYARD WILL HELP COOL THE AIR, AND THE ENCLOSURE WILL PREVENT THE LOSS OF THAT COOL AIR.

LIVING AREAS

POOL

COURT

PLAN OF HOUSE WITH COURT AND POOL, VENEZUELA

REMOVING HEAT SOURCES

ONE VERY SIMPLE WAY TO COOL A HOME IS NOT TO HEAT IT. THIS MEANS TRYING TO REMOVE THE THERMAL IMPACT OF SUCH PRIMARY FUNCTIONS AS COOKING AND BATHING.

FOR CENTURIES ONE APPROACH HAS BEEN TO REMOVE THE COOKING WORK FROM THE HOUSE AND TO CREATE A SEPARATE SUMMER KITCHEN.

SUMMER KITCHEN, CURTENI, RUMANIA

PLAN OF A FARMHOUSE IN PENNSYLVANIA (1709)

HERE, THE KITCHEN IS ATTACHED BUT NOT WITHIN THE LIVING AREA OF THE HOUSE.

CHIMNEYS ARE MAJOR HEAT SOURCES. SEPARATING THEM FROM THE HOUSE LESSENS THEIR EFFECT AND ALSO REDUCES THE FIRE HAZARD.

PARISH MANSION, VIRGINIA

TO HELP COOL HOMES TODAY, THE HEAT PRODUCED BY APPLIANCES SUCH AS STOVES, REFRIGERATORS, CLOTHES DRYERS, AND WATER HEATERS SHOULD BE KEPT AWAY FROM THE LIVING AREAS.

STAYING HEALTHY

PEOPLE HAVE ALWAYS HAD TO DEFEND THEMSELVES AGAINST THE ENVIRONMENT. THEIR SHELTERS QUICKLY BECAME THEIR PRIMARY DEFENSE. IT GAVE REFUGE FROM PESTS, PREDATORS, AND HUMANS.

THIS TREE DWELLING PROVIDES AN ESCAPE FROM THE LEECHES ON THE WET GROUND.

SAKAI TREE HOUSE, MALAYA

GROUPING DWELLINGS IN PROTECTIVE CIRCLES IS ANOTHER WAY OF GAINING SECURITY AND PRIVACY.

PLAN OF GARUNSI COMPOUND UPPER VOLTA

THIS JAPANESE PORTABLE FRAME WITH MOSQUITO NETTING PROTECTS INFANTS VERY EFFECTIVELY.

IN THE ALPS, MOST OF THE FOOD STORAGE BUILDINGS ARE RAISED ON PIERS INCORPORATING FLAT ROCKS AS RODENT GUARDS.

SOME SPECIES OF ANT HAVE SPECIAL DOORKEEPERS WITH ENLARGED HEADS. THEY PLUG THE ENTRANCES AND ADMIT ONLY THE RESIDENTS, WHO KNOW THE PROPER ANTENNA TAP CODE.

THE EAGLE USES ITS
AERIE AS A SECURE REFUGE
FROM PREDATORS AND AS AN
OBSERVATION POST FROM
WHICH TO KEEP A SHARP
EYE ON ITS DOMAIN.

LIKE THE EAGLE,
MAN OFTEN BUILT
REFUGES IN HIGH,
STRATEGIC
POSITIONS.

EAGLE'S AERIE

THE ANASAZI INDIANS
OF THE AMERICAN SOUTHWEST
USED LOFTY CRAGS IN SHEER
CLIFFS AS DEFENSIVE POSI-
TIONS AND LOOKOUTS, WHILE
THE RIVER PLAIN WAS LEFT
OPEN FOR AGRICULTURE.

THE WHITE HOUSE
CANYON DE CHELLY
ARIZONA

KUMAMOTO CASTLE, JAPAN

WHEN LACKING A
LOFTY SITE FOR A
BASTION, THE NEXT BEST
THING WAS TO CREATE A
HILL, USUALLY WITH
TIERED, FORMIDABLE
WALLS.

In Medieval Europe there was a pronounced need for fortifications. In some villages, defensive towers became a dominant architectural feature.

Village in the Caucasus U.S.S.R.

A maze of narrow, winding streets would make anyone attacking very vulnerable as they moved through the city.

San Gimignano, Italy

Mont-Saint Michel France

Limited access and narrow, winding streets gave Mt.-St. Michel a strong defense.

Harman, Rumania

Some entire villages became walled fortresses.

THE USE OF MORE
DURABLE MATERIALS IS A
VERY IMPORTANT PART OF A STRONG
DEFENSE. IN THIS CASTLE WALL,
FOR INSTANCE, THE RESISTANCE
TO FIRE IS INCREASED WITH THE
USE OF TILE, PLASTER, AND
STONE.

HIMEJI CASTLE, JAPAN

IN THE SAME CASTLE,
SOME OF THE DOORWAYS ARE
METAL-CLAD AND THUS
IMPREGNABLE.

IN 1702 THE TINDER-LIKE
THATCH AND BOARD HOUSES IN THE
SPANISH SETTLEMENT OF ST. AUGUSTINE
WERE BURNED TO THE GROUND BY
CAROLINA COLONISTS. IN REBUILDING
THE TOWN, TABBY, A MIXTURE OF
LIME MORTAR AND
SHELLS, WAS USED
TO MAKE THE
BUILDINGS MORE
RESISTANT
TO FIRE.

THATCH AND BOARD
HOUSE, ST. AUGUSTINE,
FLORIDA (1700)

TABBY AND SHINGLE HOUSE
ST. AUGUSTINE,
FLORIDA (1710)

PROTECTING THE WINDOWS:

SOLID EXTERIOR SHUTTER
PENNSYLVANIA

(SHUTTERS
SLIDE
INTO
WALL)

SLIDING INDIAN SHUTTERS
NEW HAMPSHIRE

PROTECTING AGAINST INTRUDERS

THIS INGENIOUS FLOOR HAS SPECIAL CLAMPS IN WHICH THE FLOORING NAILS CAN SLIDE, PRODUCING A CHIRPING SOUND. ANYONE WALKING ON THE FLOOR WOULD CAUSE THE CHIRPING AND THUS NO ONE COULD SNEAK UP ON THE EMPEROR

NIGHTINGALE FLOOR NIJO CASTLE, JAPAN

ONE OF THE BEST SECURITY MEASURES IS TO DESIGN THE ENTRANCE TO A DWELLING SO THAT ANYONE COMING IN IS PRACTICALLY DEFENSELESS.

MANY AFRICAN DWELLINGS' DOORWAYS HAVE HIGH THRESHOLDS AND LOW LINTELS, WHICH FORCE PEOPLE TO BOW AS THEY ENTER. THIS PUTS THEM IN A VULNERABLE POSITION.

ANOTHER EFFECTIVE WAY TO LIMIT ACCESS IS TO REMOVE THE MEANS. THIS DRAWBRIDGE CAN BE WITHDRAWN INTO THE CASTLE.

ROTHESAY CASTLE SCOTLAND (1312)

EARLY PUEBLO DWELLINGS HAD LADDERS THROUGH THE ROOF FOR ACCESS. THE LADDER COULD BE DRAWN UP FOR SECURITY. ENTERING BY DESCENDING A LADDER ALSO MADE AN INTRUDER VERY VULNERABLE.

SECTION THROUGH ACOMA PUEBLO, NEW MEXICO (A.D. 900)

METAL DOOR AND WINDOW GRILLES CAN BAR ACCESS BUT STILL ADMIT LIGHT AND AIR.

WINDOW GRILLE, VENEZUELA

SLEEPING

Due to poor night vision, people are very vulnerable creatures in the dark, so early shelters were simply protected places in which to sleep. Very soon, though, builders went beyond crude shelter and began to pay attention to comfort.

NEOLITHIC DWELLING
KÖLN LINDENTHAL, GERMANY
THE EARTH FLOOR WAS SCULPTED TO CREATE SEATS, BEDS, ETC.

INUIT IGLOO, CANADA

The air at the top of a space is warmer (warm air rises), so sleeping shelves in igloos are built up off the floor.

In some Japanese homes a pit, or RO, containing hot coals is covered by a wooden frame and is used to preheat the bedding, or futon.

Some masonry stoves have built-in platforms that can be used as cozy sleeping shelves.

Traditional Finnish stove with grandmother shelf.

In other areas staying cool is a primary goal, and often the roof becomes a cool and safe sleeping loft.

GARUNSI HUT, UPPER VOLTA

In Japan the bedding, or futon, is stored in a closet, or "oshiire," and brought out as needed at night. This saves space, because during the day no room is just an unused bedroom, and at night any room can become a bedroom.

Closet ("oshiire") for storing futons Japan

Over the centuries people have devised many ingenious ways to secrete beds for privacy, security, or just aesthetics.

Two-tiered Breton cupboard bed with sliding doors.

Partitioned and curtained bed alcove.

Holland, 17th century

The two small lean-tos at either side of this house were added as extra sleeping spaces.

Nantucket Whaler's House, 18th century

COOKING

EARLY SHELTERS WERE SIMPLY
FOR SLEEPING, BUT IN COOLER
CLIMATES THERE WAS A NEED TO BRING
THE FIRE INSIDE TO COOK AND ADD
WARMTH. THE EARLIEST HEARTHS
CONSISTED OF SIMPLE OPEN
FIREPITS, FROM WHICH THE
FIREPLACE EVOLVED.

EARLY JAPANESE SAND HEARTH
WITH KETTLE ARM

NORWEGIAN FIREPLACE WITH
ADJUSTABLE KETTLE HOLDER

JAPANESE
KETTLE HOLDER
(THE WOOD BLOCK ON THE
ROPE LOCKS THE HEIGHT
ADJUSTMENT)

WOOD
BLOCK

JAPANESE CHARCOAL
FIREPLACE

AS THE FIREPLACE BECAME INTEGRATED INTO THE STRUCTURE OF THE HOUSE A HOOD WAS BUILT TO CAPTURE THE SMOKE, AND THE FIREPLACE GREW INTO A DOMINANT CENTRAL ELEMENT.

PLAN OF AN ENGLISH FIREPLACE (1500's)

THE HOOD OVER THIS FIRE-PLACE COVERS BOTH THE FIRE AND AN INGLENOOK, WHICH HAS A SMALL WINDOW. ONE SIDE OF THE HOOD IS SUPPORTED BY A SHORT WALL CALLED A HECK, WHICH ALSO BUFFERS THE ENTRY.

THIS CORNER FIREPLACE HAS A HOOD OF WATTLE AND DAUB (SEE PAGE 121) SUPPORTED BY A LINTEL THAT WAS MADE FROM THE CROOK OF A TREE.

DOUBLE-ARCHED, MASSIVE CORNER FIREPLACE TAOS, NEW MEXICO (1834)

ARCHED HOOD LIVING ROOM FIREPLACE, COPENHAGEN

GRADUALLY THE OPEN FIREPLACE
EVOLVED INTO AN ENCLOSED
FIREBOX THAT WAS MUCH
MORE EFFICIENT AT TRANS-
FERRING HEAT TO THE
COOKING VESSELS.

THE SPANISH
MASONRY STOVE, OR FOGÓN,
HAS SEVERAL SMALL FIRE-
BOXES UNDER A TILE
COOKING SURFACE.

SPANISH FOGÓN
ST. AUGUSTINE, FLORIDA
(1787)

A HOOD TO CARRY OFF THE SMOKE
WAS A WELCOME ADDITION.

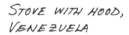

STOVE WITH HOOD,
VENEZUELA

EARLY JAPANESE STOVES
HAD COOKING RECESSES AND A
RICE STEAMER.

JAPANESE STOVE

THE AUSTRIAN KACHELOFEN
DOUBLES AS A COOKSTOVE
AND THE MAIN SOURCE
OF HEAT. ITS TILES
HOLD HEAT FOR
LONG PERIODS.

AUSTRIAN KACHELOFEN

INDIAN OVEN,
OKLAHOMA

THE HEMISPHERICAL OVEN
EXPOSES A MINIMUM OF SURFACE
AREA FOR HEAT LOSS (SEE PAGE 27),
AND IT ALSO GIVES A VERY EVEN
RADIANT HEAT WITHIN. THESE
REASONS, PLUS THE FACT THAT IT IS
EASY TO BUILD, HAVE MADE IT THE
FAVORED FORM FOR CENTURIES.

DOGON OVEN
UPPER VOLTA

STONE

ADOBE

PUEBLO INDIAN PIKI OVEN
NEW MEXICO

A SMALL FIRE INSIDE HEATS THE
STONE SLAB FOR COOKING
PIKI WAFERS.

THE SHAKERS BUILT
LARGE OVENS WITH SEVERAL
REVOLVING RACKS FOR HIGH-VOLUME
BAKING.

SHAKER OVEN
CANTERBURY, NEW HAMPSHIRE
(1876)

A SHEET METAL REFLECTOR OVEN
FOCUSES A FIRE'S HEAT ONTO
THE RACK AT ITS
CENTER.

OVEN   FIRE

REFLECTOR OVEN
MASSACHUSETTS, 18th CENTURY

JAPANESE TEAPOT
THIS TEAPOT HAS AN EFFICIENT AND
PRACTICAL SHAPE: MAXIMUM SURFACE AREA EXPOSED
TO THE STOVE'S HEAT AND THE MINIMUM AREA EXPOSED
TO THE AIR (DUE TO THE HEMISPHERICAL SHAPE)

EATING

THE USE OF TABLES, CHAIRS, AND
UTENSILS FOR DINING HAS
OCCURRED ONLY IN THE
LAST SEVERAL CENTU-
RIES AND, IN MANY
COUNTRIES, IS EVEN NOW
NOT OBSERVED.

HOUSE OF CARO, POMPEII

THIS HOUSE HAS
A U-SHAPED INCLINED
DAIS THAT WAS USED FOR
DINING. THE FOOD WAS
SERVED FROM THE
CENTER AREA.

SECTION THROUGH DAIS AND
SERVICE AREA

IN SOME OLDER JAPANESE HOMES THERE IS
A RECESS, OR "HORIGOTATSU," IN THE FLOOR
UNDER THE TABLE INTO WHICH HOT COALS
ARE PLACED TO WARM THE FEET
OF THE DINERS.

JAPANESE "HORIGOTATSU"

THE SEATING ARRANGEMENT
IN THE ANCIENT MONESTARY ON
MT. ATHOS ACCOMMODATES LARGE
NUMBERS OF PEOPLE AND
ALLOWS EASY SERVICE ACCESS
AT THE END OF THE
TABLE.

EATING TABLES AT THE MONESTARY
ON MT. ATHOS, GREECE (A.D. 950)

THE FRONT OF THIS
CUPBOARD SWINGS DOWN
TO MAKE A TABLE.

CUPBOARD/TABLE, ALPS

SITTING

Even in Neolithic times, builders were creating raised platforms for sitting, working, and sleeping.

At Çatal Hüyük the plastered dais was covered with mats, cushions, and bedding.

ÇATAL HÜYÜK ANATOLIA (6000 B.C.)

African villages very often have a shaded resting place where people can quietly gather and chat or just sit.

RESTING PLACE, DAHOMEY

UR PLATFORM, CHINA

This is used as a dais for sitting and reclining.

Raised sections of the floor in many Japanese buildings are used for sitting.

THE THREE-LEGGED STOOL

ON VERY UNEVEN FLOORS IT STILL SITS FLAT.

JAPANESE PAVILION SHUGAKUIN IMPERIAL VILLA

BATHING

As the house evolved from a crude shelter into a home, bathing received more attention.

This terra-cotta hip bath was found in an elaborately tiled bathroom.

HIP BATH, OLYNTHUS (A.D. 300)

The long drain spout on this triangular terra-cotta sink extended through the wall and emptied into a sewer.

BASIN, OLYNTHUS, GREECE
(A.D. 300)

The use of portable tubs saves the space taken up by a permanent bathroom and allows one to bathe in the warmth of the kitchen.

SHAKER BATHING TUB
SABBATHDAY LAKE, MAINE (1878)

Early Japanese tubs were made of wood with a metal-shielded bottom under which a fire was built.

JAPANESE BATH TUB

Older Japanese homes kept the heat and messy fire of the bath separated from the living areas. The toilet was also separate, but for a different reason.

TOILET   KITCHEN
STORAGE
LIVING
AREA
PORCH   ENTRANCE   BATH

WHEN POSSIBLE, MOST DOMESTIC
ACTIVITIES IN HOT CLIMATES ARE
DONE OUTSIDE, INCLUDING
BATHING.

WASHING ENCLOSURES
SHORT WALL

PLAN OF
GARUNSI
COMPOUND
UPPER VOLTA

FOR PRIVACY WHILE
WASHING, LOW-WALLED
CUBICLES ARE ATTACHED
TO THESE DWELLING
COMPLEXES BUILT
OF MUD.

IN JAPAN, BATHING
RECEIVES A GREAT DEAL OF
ATTENTION AND IS PRACTICALLY
AN ART FORM.
   AS SHOWN IN THIS CONTEMPORARY
PLAN, THE JAPANESE BELIEVE IN
SEPARATING THE BATH AND
THE TOILET.

TOILET
TUB
TILE FLOOR
WITH DRAIN

CONTEMPORARY BATH PLAN, JAPAN

ON THE OTHER HAND, THE JAPANESE
HAVE ALSO PRODUCED ONE-PIECE,
PLUG-IN, FIBERGLASS
BATHROOM MODULES.

JAPANESE UNITIZED BATHROOM

   SOME EARLY WOOD-FIRED
JAPANESE TUBS WERE INSIDE WHILE
THE FIRE WAS OUTSIDE. THE WATER
CIRCULATED THROUGH PORTS IN THE WALL.

TUB
FIRE

THE JAPANESE WASH
OUTSIDE OF THE TUB, EITHER BY
LADLING OUT WATER OR USING A
SHOWER NOZZLE, AND THEN THEY GET
IN THE TUB TO SOAK. THE SAME
WATER CAN BE USED SEVERAL
TIMES AND A CIRCULATING
HEATER KEEPS IT VERY HOT.

HEATER
HOT
COOL

ELIMINATION

With the establishment of more permanent shelters came the need for a system to deal with sewage. For centuries in China, human waste has been considered a very valuable commodity. It is collected, composted, aged, and then used as a high-quality fertilizer, called night soil.

One of the more primitive waste disposal systems is the outhouse.

The outhouse is simply a sewer pit topped by an enclosed toilet seat. Periodically lime is added to the pit to reduce odors and when it is full it is covered with earth, a new pit is dug, and the outhouse is placed over it.

SEAT

PIT

NEW YORK (CA. 1910)

Where to situate the outhouse:
1) Put it downwind from the house,
2) Keep it away from any water sources,
3) Place the woodpile between it and the house so that commuters can bring in some wood on their return trip.

WELL

HOUSE

WOODPILE

OUTHOUSE

PREVAILING WIND

Indoor facilities:

TOILET

MARMOT SUMMER BURROW

When the marmot excavates its burrow it digs a short, spur tunnel that is used as a toilet.

In 3000 B.C. the residents of Olynthus had an underground, brick-lined sewer system that even had lines serving each sentry's post on the city wall.

FEEDER LINE

MAIN

OLYNTHUS, GREECE

IN COLD CLIMATES, A TREK TO THE OUTHOUSE IS NOT TOO POPULAR, SO OFTEN A PRIVY IS BUILT INTO A CORNER OF THE BARN.

"DAS STILLE ÖRTCHEN"
(LIT. "THE SMALLEST ROOM")
MATTEN, SWITZERLAND
(17ᵗᴴ CENTURY)

TOILET MADE FROM AN OLD BUTTER CHURN

THE TOILET WAS FIRST BROUGHT INTO THE HOUSE AS SIMPLY A BUCKET WITH A SEAT. THE BUCKET WAS EMPTIED DAILY AT THE DUNG HEAP.

SWITZERLAND
(1693)

PERSONAL HYGIENE HAS ALWAYS BEEN VERY IMPORTANT TO THE JAPANESE, WHICH IS EVIDENT IN THE FIXTURES THAT THEY HAVE DEVELOPED.

MOST OF THE WORLD'S CULTURES FAVOR THE SQUAT-TYPE TOILET BECAUSE IT IS SIMPLE, IT PROMOTES A NATURAL POSITION, AND IT IS VERY SANITARY.

JAPANESE PRIVY (CA. 1870)

THIS MODERN JAPANESE TOILET HAS TWO WATER-SAVING FEATURES: 1) WITH ITS DUAL FLUSH MODE, LITTLE OR MORE WATER CAN BE USED AS NECESSARY, AND 2) WATER REFILLING THE TANK CAN BE USED FOR WASHING ONE'S HANDS.

SPOUT

TANK

CONTEMPORARY JAPANESE TOILET

JAPANESE URINAL, OR "ASAGAOWA"
(LIT. "MORNING FACE"; IT IS SUPPOSED TO RESEMBLE THE FLOWER OF THE MORNING GLORY) (CA. 1870)

Working

As civilization went beyond the hunting/gathering phase and the complexity of domestic life increased, it became important to have space in the shelter for necessary tasks and for storage.

PLAN

Muktele House, Cameroon

The circular compound of huts projects and defines an inner yard that is used as an outdoor living area, a work space, and a safe place to store things.

The flat roof has been used in a variety of climates for centuries as a practical and safe place for working, sleeping, drying produce, and keeping animals.

Mountain Settlement Andalusia, Spain

Acoma Pueblo New Mexico (ca. A.D. 900)

In many areas, the shape of the house is manipulated to create both open and shaded exterior areas.

Under these vaults are shaded outdoor living and working areas.

Ostuni, Italy

EARLY DWELLINGS IN TEMPERATE CLIMATES USUALLY HOUSED ALL ACTIVITIES UNDER ONE ROOF TO CONSERVE HEAT.

ENGLISH LONGHOUSE (PRE-1100)

SOME LATER HOMES SPLIT THE DWELLING AND THE BYRE AND CREATED A PROTECTED, PARTIALLY COVERED COURT BETWEEN THEM THAT SERVED A VARIETY OF USES.

FRENCH FARMHOUSE PLAN

THE PROJECTING ROOF AND SIDE WALLS OF THIS BARN CREATE A PROTECTED OUTSIDE WORK AREA.

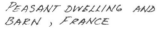

PEASANT DWELLING AND BARN, FRANCE

NEW ENGLAND BUILDERS CONNECT THE BARN AND HOUSE WITH A CHAIN OF WORK SPACES. THIS MINIMIZES THE NECESSITY OF GOING OUTSIDE IN WINTER.

NEW ENGLAND FARMHOUSE (CA. 1800)

LOGGIAS PROVIDE LIVING AND WORKING SPACE THAT IS SHELTERED FROM BOTH THE RAIN AND THE SUN.

COURT AND LOGGIA, GREECE

STORAGE

CULTIVATION OF CROPS BEGAN AT LEAST 10,000 YEARS AGO AND WITH THIS SHIFT TO AN AGRARIAN SOCIETY CAME THE NEED TO STORE FOOD. THE GRANARY BECAME THE MOST IMPORTANT BUILDING IN THE SETTLEMENT.

CLAY POT GRANARY, SUDAN

THE GRANARY WAS USUALLY THE FIRST STRUCTURE BUILT IN A SETTLEMENT AND WAS THE MOST METICULOUSLY CRAFTED.

MUD AND THATCH GRANARY, MEXICO

THIS ELABORATELY CARVED STONE GRANARY HAS LARGE FLAT STONES AT THE TOP OF EACH SUPPORTING POST AS A RAT GUARD.

STONE GRANARY GALICIA, SPAIN

LARGE WOODEN GRANARY
ELMALI, TURKEY   (19ᵗʰ CENTURY)

"KURA", JAPAN
(CA. 1800)

THE IMPORTANCE OF
RICE TO THE JAPANESE
IS CLEARLY EVIDENT
FROM A LOOK AT THE TILE
AND STUCCO, FIREPROOF
STRUCTURE, OR "KURA,"
WHERE IT IS STORED.
THIS FORTRESS-LIKE
BUILDING PROTECTS THE
RICE FROM BOTH
MOISTURE AND FIRE.

DETAIL OF THE VAULT-
TYPE DOOR ON A
"KURA."

RAISED STOREHOUSE, FINLAND

THIS ELEVATED STRUCTURE,
OUT OF THE REACH OF SNOW
AND ANIMALS, SERVES AS A
STOREHOUSE AND TEMPORARY
SHELTER FOR
THE LAPPS.

CORN CRIBS USUALLY
HAVE OPEN, SLATTED WALLS
TO ALLOW AIR TO FLOW THROUGH
AND DRY THE CORN. SOME
HAVE ADDITIONAL STORM FLAPS
TO KEEP OUT DRIVING RAIN.
    IN THIS EXAMPLE NOTE
THE RAT GUARDS ON THE
POSTS AND THE STEP THAT
IS RETRACTED WITH A
COUNTERWEIGHT TO PREVENT
ANIMALS FROM REACHING
THE CORN.

HIGHRISE STOREHOUSE
MEDENINE, TUNISIA

ROOT CELLAR
QUEBEC (1650)

ROOT CELLARS
WERE USUALLY BUILT
ABOVE GROUND TO STAY DRY AND
THEN EARTH WAS PILED OVER
THEM TO MAINTAIN A
CONSTANT, COOL
TEMPERATURE FOR
STORING POTATOES, BEETS,
TURNIPS, ETC.

ROOT CELLAR UNDER BARN RAMP
PENNSYLVANIA (1830)

A WET GROUND-CELLAR IS
AN UNDERGROUND STOREROOM
ADJOINING A WELL. POOLS OF
WELL WATER COOLED MILK,
CIDER, ETC.

SPRINGHOUSES KEEP THE
SPRING WATER CLEAN AND SUPPLY
A POOL OF COOL RUNNING WATER
TO CHILL MILK, ETC.

SPRINGHOUSE, PENNSYLVANIA (CA. 1800)

SECTION THROUGH THE STONE WALL OF A TRULLO DWELLING SHOWING A BUILT-IN STORAGE NICHE

APULIA, ITALY

A SIMPLE AND VERSATILE WAY TO STORE CLOTHES IS IN A WARDROBE, THESE MOVABLE PIECES ARE STILL VERY POPULAR IN EUROPE.

THE JAPANESE ARE NOTED FOR THEIR SIMPLE YET ELEGANT DESIGNS, SUCH AS THIS UTENSIL HOLDER, MADE OF NOTCHED BAMBOO.

THE SHAKERS TRULY BELIEVE IN "A PLACE FOR EVERYTHING, AND EVERYTHING IN ITS PLACE." THIS SERIES OF ATTIC CLOSETS AND DRAWERS IN CANTERBURY, N.H. ATTESTS TO THAT.

ANOTHER FAVORITE STORAGE METHOD WAS TO HANG THINGS ON PEGS ON THE WALLS.

ADJUSTABLE CANDLE HOLDER

SHELVES

CHAIR (HUNG UPSIDE DOWN TO KEEP DUST OFF THE SEAT)

SECTION III - THE BUILDING ITSELF

Regionality

Over the course of history, the environment has been the strongest determinant of what form shelter will take. In order to be successful, a shelter must be built to counter local negative environmental conditions, and it must be constructed with available materials. These two factors are chiefly responsible for the distinctly regional quality of pre-industrial indigenous architecture. This section of the book examines the materials and techniques that builders used to achieve the goals mentioned in the previous sections.

IRELAND: TEMPERATE CLIMATE, STONE AND THATCH AVAILABLE

SIBERIA: COLD CLIMATE, WOOD AVAILABLE

NEW MEXICO: WARM, ARID CLIMATE, CLAY AVAILABLE FOR ADOBE

ARABIA: DESERT CLIMATE, WOOL AVAILABLE FOR CLOTH

INDONESIA: HOT AND HUMID CLIMATE, PLANT MATERIALS AVAILABLE

USING THE MATERIALS AT HAND

PALM FRONDS AND GRASS SUPPLY WEAVERBIRDS WITH THE MATERIALS NECESSARY TO CREATE THEIR INTRICATELY WOVEN, SPHERICAL NESTS.

THE EARLIEST MAN-MADE SHELTER WAS MOST LIKELY A ROOF OF STICKS, BRANCHES, AND LEAVES BRIDGING A TROUGH IN THE TERRAIN.

THIS ABORIGINAL SHELTER IN CENTRAL AUSTRALIA IS MADE OF ARCHED BRANCHES WITH A LEAF COVERING. THE FLOOR IS SLIGHTLY SCOOPED OUT.

THE BAMBUTI PEOPLE OF THE ITURI FOREST IN THE CONGO USE LARGE LEAVES TO COVER TWIG FRAMES AS A SIMPLE SHELTER.

THE DINKA TRIBE OF THE UPPER NILE USES SOME LOCAL MATERIALS IN PLACE. THE TWIG AND THATCH ROOF OF THIS HUT IS SUPPORTED BY THE TRIMMED BRANCHES OF A TREE.

ON LAKE TITICACA, IN PERU, THE URUS INDIANS HAVE USED TOTORA REEDS TO CREATE FLOATING ISLANDS UPON WHICH THEY BUILD THEIR HOUSES. THE HOUSES THEMSELVES ARE ALSO BUILT ENTIRELY OF REEDS.

THIS PRIMITIVE AUSTRALIAN HUT IS MADE OF LARGE SHEETS OF BARK BENT OVER A SIMPLE STICK FRAME.

FOR CENTURIES, THE JAPANESE HAVE BEEN DISPLAYING THEIR MASTERY OF THE CRAFT OF THATCHING.

TAKAYAMA, JAPAN

THE BOUND BUNDLES OF STRAW CAN BE MADE INTO ROOFS (ABOVE) OR WALLS (LEFT). THATCH IS USED THROUGHOUT THE WORLD BECAUSE GRASS IS SO UNIVERSALLY AVAILABLE AND IS REPLENISHABLE.

IN NORWAY, SOD HAS LONG BEEN USED AS A DURABLE, INSULATING ROOF MATERIAL. IT IS OFTEN PLACED OVER A LAYER OF BARK, WHICH KEEPS WATER FROM SEEPING INTO THE HOUSE.

SOD
BARK
WOOD
SECTION THROUGH ROOF

LOG HOUSE
WITH
SOD ROOF

OSTERDAL, NORWAY (17th CENTURY)

THE WELL-DIGGER JAWFISH
BUILDS A HIDEAWAY FROM WHICH TO
STRIKE AT PREY BY DIGGING A HOLE
AND REINFORCING IT WITH
PEBBLES AND SHELLS.

PERHAPS THE EARLIEST
FORM OF MAN-MADE STONE
BUILDING IS THE DOLMEN:
A STRUCTURE OF STONE
SLABS USED AS A
BURIAL CHAMBER.

THIS PRE-DYNASTIC EGYPTIAN
HOUSE WAS CREATED WITHIN
A BOULDER FORMATION.

THIS TRULLO DWELLING
IS BUILT OF UNMORTARED
STONE, WHICH IS CORBELED
TO CREATE A VAULTED
INTERIOR.

MURGIA, ITALY
(CA. 1600)

THE MOST WIDELY AVAILABLE BUILDING MATERIAL IS THE EARTH ITSELF. FOR MILLIONS OF YEARS, ANIMALS HAVE BEEN LIVING IN BURROWS FOR PROTECTION FROM COLD, HEAT, MOISTURE, AND PREDATORS.

MANY BURROWS ARE EVEN EQUIPPED WITH SHORT TUNNELS USED AS BATHROOMS.

SECTION OF A MARMOT'S SUMMER BURROW

3,000 YEARS AGO, PEOPLE CARVED BURIAL CHAMBERS INTO THESE CLIFFS OF SOFT ROCK. DURING THE MIDDLE AGES THEY WERE CONVERTED INTO DWELLINGS.

CARVED CLIFF HOUSES, ANAPO VALLEY, SICILY

IN NORTHERN CHINA, A VERY LARGE NUMBER OF PEOPLE LIVE IN SUBTERRANEAN DWELLINGS CARVED INTO THE LOESS SOIL AND RADIATING FROM SUNKEN COURTYARDS.

UNDERGROUND DWELLINGS NEAR LO-YANG, NO. CHINA

MANY ELABORATE, MULTILEVEL DWELLINGS HAVE BEEN CARVED FROM THE SOFT TUFA CONES OF CAPPADOCIA.

CAPPADOCIA, TURKEY

ANOTHER WAY TO USE
EARTH FOR SHELTER IS
TO CUT SOD BLOCKS
AND USE THEM LIKE
BRICKS TO BUILD
WALLS.

SOD HOUSE
AMERICAN MIDWEST
(CA. 1840)

THE ANIMALS HUNTED
BY THE PLAINS INDIANS
SUPPLIED THEM WITH
FOOD AND SHELTER.
THE DEMOUNTABLE POLE
FRAMES OF THEIR TEPEES
ARE COVERED INSIDE
AND OUT WITH
HIDES.

AMERICAN PLAINS INDIAN TEPEE

THE TEKNA TRIBES OF SOUTHWEST
MOROCCO USE THE HAIR
FROM SHEEP, GOATS, AND
CAMELS AS THE RAW
MATERIAL FOR THEIR
TENTS. THESE PORTABLE
AND EASILY ERECTED
TENTS ARE WELL SUITED TO
THE TEKNA'S NOMADIC
LIFESTYLE.

TEKNA TENT
MOROCCO

IN A SUB-ARCTIC CLIMATE,
SNOW IS ONE OF THE FEW
MATERIALS AVAILABLE.
MANY TRIBES HAVE USED
SNOW BLOCKS IN CON-
STRUCTION FOR CENTURIES.
THE BLOCKS, EASILY CUT
AND SHAPED, ARE LAID IN
A SPIRALING PATTERN.

INUIT IGLOO
CANADA

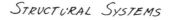

STRUCTURAL SYSTEMS

OUR PALEOLITHIC ANCESTORS MIGHT HAVE TAKEN REFUGE IN SOME NATURAL LEAN-TO SHELTERS OF TREES FALLEN AGAINST A BANK OR ACCROSS A GULLY.

LATER, THEY LEARNED HOW TO BUILD THEM THEMSELVES.

THE NEXT STEP MAY HAVE BEEN A LEAN-TO ROOF RESTING ON A CROSSBAR.

THE MORE COMMON, CIRCULAR DWELLING MAY HAVE ORIGINATED WITH A LEAN-TO RADIATING FROM A TREE.

NEOLITHIC MAN BUILT PITHOUSES THAT HAD A CIRCULAR FRAME ROOF OVER A SHALLOW PIT.

MUD
STICKS

PITHOUSE, PAN-P'O, CHINA (4000 B.C.)

THE RECTANGULAR PITHOUSE WAS A MORE RATIONAL FORM; THE CIRCULAR WAS MORE INTUITIVE.

TENCHI-GONGEN PITHOUSE, JAPAN

THE NEXT PHASE WAS THE DIFFERENTIATION OF WALL AND ROOF.

WOODEN CRUCK

ENGLISH CRUCK BUILDING (1500)

STONE STRUCTURES

STONE
EARTH

TRULLO HOUSE, MURGIA, ITALY (1400's)

MORTARLESS STONE VAULTING
APPEARED IN EGYPT AND MESOPOTAMIA
BEFORE 3000 B.C. AND WAS OF THE
CORBELED, TRULLO TYPE.

CORBELED
STONEWORK

THE AEGEAN CULTURES
OF GREECE AND CRETE MADE
EXTENSIVE USE OF THE STONE
LINTEL BECAUSE OF THE
DURABLE STONE AVAILABLE
TO THEM.

STONE LINTEL, GREECE

THE TRIANGULAR ARCH MARKED A TRANSITION
FROM THE LINTEL TO THE ARCH.

WINDOW LINTEL, TIGRÉ HOUSE
ETHIOPIA

VAULTED, UNMORTARED
STONE STRUCTURES
APPEARED IN
EUROPE ALSO.

STONE ORATORY, IRELAND
(6th OR 7th CENTURY)

A COMMON BUILDING TYPE IS A
MIXTURE OF MASSIVE STONE
WALLS AND A LIGHT, EASILY
CONSTRUCTED FRAME AND
THATCH ROOF.

FARMHOUSE, SCOTLAND (18th CENTURY)

THE STICKLEBACK FISH BUILDS A VAULTED NEST BY CONSTRUCTING A SOLID, SEMI-CYLINDRICAL MASS OF PLANT MATERIAL AND THEN TUNNELING A HOLE THROUGH IT.

FOR CENTURIES, VARIOUS CULTURES HAVE USED PLANT MATERIALS TO FRAME AND COVER VAULTS.

INDIAN FRAME VAULT, AMERICA

VAULT FRAMED WITH JOINED BUNDLES OF REEDS AND COVERED WITH REED MATS, IRAQ

AIRSHIP HANGAR, FRANCE (1916)

MORE RECENTLY, CONCRETE HAS BEEN USED TO BUILD THIN-SHELLED VAULTS

CONTEMPORARY DOMES ARE OFTEN OF PRECAST CONCRETE SECTIONS BOUND BY A BAND, OR TENSION RING, AROUND THE PERIMETER.

CONCRETE DOME, VIRGINIA (1964)

KHOISAN HUT SOUTH AFRICA

A VERY ANCIENT, INTUITIVE HOUSE FORM IS THE DOME, OR BEEHIVE SHAPE.

POST AND LINTEL

It is easy to see how the later Greek monumental architecture evolved from this simple, primitive hut, which has tree trunk posts and timber roof framing.

GREEK HUT (PRE-3000 B.C.)

The capital atop each column spreads the support of the column along the architrave.

ARCHITRAVE →

CAPITAL { ABACUS ECHINUS }

COLUMN →

Ancient examples of stone construction using massive lintel blocks can be found throughout Central and South America.

MACHU PICCHU, PERU (CA. 1500)

Where posts and beams are used in Pueblo architecture, a zapata is usually added, like a capital, to spread the support of the post.

SANTA FE, NEW MEXICO (CA. 1860)

In Holland, wood post and beam construction is used to support masonry walls while providing large openings for store windows.

AMSTERDAM, HOLLAND (CA. 1850)

THE FRAME

A FRAME STRUCTURAL SYSTEM WITH A SKIN OF ROOF AND WALLS HAS SEVERAL ADVANTAGES OVER SOLID BUILDINGS. IT IS LIGHTER, CAN BE ASSEMBLED MORE QUICKLY, IS OFTEN DEMOUNTABLE, USES MATERIALS MORE ECONOMICALLY, IS EASY TO ALTER AND EXPAND, AND CAN FLEX TO RESIST EARTHQUAKES.

MURO-JI SHRINE
JAPAN

FRAME OF
BOUND POLES
VENEZUELA

TIMBER FRAME WITH
CORNER BRACING

MORTISE

TENON

POST   WOOD PEG,
OR TRUNNEL

BEAM

MORTISE AND TENON JOINT

THE CORNER BRACING HELPS A FRAME STRUCTURE TO RESIST LATERAL FORCES SUCH AS WIND AND EARTHQUAKES (SEE PAGE 25).

THE HALF-TIMBER STRUCTURE HAS WALLS OF STONE, BRICK, PLASTER, OR WATTLE AND DAUB (SEE PAGE 121), WHICH FILL IN THE AREAS BETWEEN THE TIMBERS, LEAVING THEM EXPOSED.

HALF-TIMBER HOUSE, DENMARK

THE CANTILEVER

THIS OVERHANGING, OR JETTIED, SECOND FLOOR ADDS SPACE UPSTAIRS AND ALSO PROTECTS THE LOWER WALL FROM THE WEATHER.

KENT, ENGLAND
(15ᵗʰ CENTURY)

THIS BRACKET, CALLED A BRESSUMMER, SUPPORTS THE JETTY.

(ENGLAND)

SIDE VIEW OF A COMPOUND BRACKET, WHICH IS COMMON IN JAPANESE ARCHITECTURE. (CA. 1500)

THIS UPPER FLOOR AREA IS CANTILEVERED OVER A RIVER AND IS SUPPORTED BY DIAGONAL BRACES.
LUXEMBOURG

OVERSHOT BARN; TENNESSEE

PENDILL

GARRISON STYLE

MASSACHUSETTS
(17ᵗʰ CENTURY)

THE POTTER WASP BUILDS
SMALL CLAY POTS TO PROTECT ITS EGGS.
IT GATHERS SMALL BALLS OF CLAY,
WHICH IT MOISTENS, FASHIONS INTO
FLAT, NARROW STRIPS, AND USES
TO BUILD UP THE WALL OF THE POT.
IT THEN LAYS AN EGG INSIDE
SUSPENDED OVER A COLLECTION OF
PARALYZED INSECTS THAT WILL BE FOOD
FOR THE LARVA. THE TOP IS THEN CORKED
WITH A BALL OF CLAY. WHEN THE YOUNG WASP IS LARGE
ENOUGH, IT BREAKS OUT OF ITS POT.

POTTER WASP
CLAY POTS

SEMI-SPHERICAL CLAY HUT
AFGHANISTAN

THE ROUND MUD HUT
OF THE MASSA TRIBE IN THE
SUDAN IS BUILT OF SUCCESSIVE
COURSES OF MUD, LAID AND
SHAPED BY HAND, FORMING
A CYLINDER AND TOPPED WITH
A THATCH ROOF.

MASSA MUD HUT
LOGONE RIVER
SUDAN

SOME STRUCTURES BUILT BY THE
HOHOKAM INDIANS OF ARIZONA
WERE CONSTRUCTED BY BUILDING UP
COURSES OF HAND-SHAPED MUD
TWO TO THREE FEET HIGH.

CASA GRANDE, ARIZONA (CA.1250)

THE SPANISH TECHNIQUE
OF USING BOARD FORMS TO HOLD
THE POURED WALL WHILE IT CURED
WAS USED IN THE CONSTRUCTION OF
TABBY WALLS. (SEE PAGE 71.)

TABBY WALL
ST. AUGUSTINE,
FLORIDA
(1750)

THE ROOF

PERHAPS THE FIRST MAN-MADE ROOF FORM WAS THE LEAN-TO. IT IS A SIMPLE, INTUITIVE ANSWER TO THE NEED FOR SHELTER.

"BANAB," OR RAIN SHELTER, OF THE SOUTHERN GUIANA INDIANS (THE FRAME GETS A COVER OF BRUSH.)

ONE OF THE EARLIEST AND SIMPLEST ROOF FORMS IS THE CONE. OF ALL THE SHAPES THAT CAN BE BUILT USING STRAIGHT MEMBERS, THE CONICAL ROOF OFFERS A MAXIMUM OF FLOOR AREA WITH A MINIMUM OF EXPOSED SURFACE AREA.

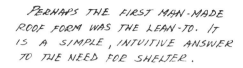

PENOBSCOT INDIAN TEPEE

USABLE LIVING SPACE CAN BE INCREASED WHEN THE CONICAL ROOF IS RAISED ON OUTER WALLS.

WAI WAI DWELLING BRITISH GUIANA

THIS EXAMPLE SHOWS AN INTERESTING COMBINATION OF GABLE AND CONICAL ROOFS. THE GABLE ALLOWS FOR A LARGE INTERIOR SPACE AND THE CONICAL ENDS MINIMIZE SURFACE EXPOSURE THERE.

JIBARO JIVARIA, ECUADOR

THE GABLE ROOF ALLOWS FOR BETTER THROUGH-VENTILATION AND ALSO PERMITS EASY LINEAR EXPANSION OF THE STRUCTURE. (A CIRCLE IS MORE DIFFICULT TO EXPAND THAN A RECTANGLE.)

SEMINOLE LODGE

104

IN SIMPLE, PRIMITIVE DWELLINGS THERE IS NO DIFFERENTIATION BETWEEN THE ROOF AND THE WALLS.

CHURUATA HUT VENEZUELA

THE CHURUATA HUT OF THE VENEZUELAN INDIANS IS MADE BY PLACING A CIRCLE OF POLES IN THE GROUND, THEN BENDING THEM INTO A DOUBLE CURVE AND BINDING THEM AT THE TOP.

MASAI HOUSE AFRICA

THE MASAI BUILD THEIR HUTS IN A SIMILAR WAY EXCEPT THAT TWIGS, WOVEN BETWEEN THE SAPLING POLES, CREATE A VERTICAL WALL, ABOVE WHICH THE SAPLINGS ARE BENT TO ARC ACROSS TO THE OTHER SIDE. THE HOUSE IS LATER PLASTERED WITH A MIXTURE OF MUD AND DUNG.

THE ADDED SUPPORTING POLES AROUND THE PERIMETER OF THIS HOUSE SUGGEST THE BEGINNINGS OF A SEPARATE WALL SYSTEM.

WICHITA INDIAN HOUSE

MARQUESAS Is. HOUSE

IN THIS HOUSE, THE WALL STRUCTURE IS PLAINLY SEPARATED FROM THE ROOF. THIS RESULTS IN THE ELIMINATION OF THE THE UNUSABLE LOW-CEILINGED SPACE AT THE PERIMETER.

HOUSE FORMS THAT AVOID THE TRANSITION FROM WALL TO ROOF ARE STILL POPULAR TODAY BECAUSE THEY ARE EASY TO BUILD, USE FEWER MATERIALS, AND OFFER GOOD PROTECTION FROM THE WEATHER.

A-FRAME HOUSE, VERMONT

SECTION THROUGH LOG DOME
MESA VERDE, COLORADO

WHERE AVAILABLE, WOOD HAS
ALWAYS BEEN A POPULAR
BUILDING MATERIAL BECAUSE IT
IS EASY TO SHAPE AND IS
RELATIVELY LIGHT. IN SOME
PRIMITIVE BUILDINGS IT
WAS LAID IN COURSES
OR CORBELED
LIKE STONEWORK.

LOG DOME, PAKISTAN
(VIEWED FROM BELOW)

BECAUSE OF ITS FIBROUS NATURE,
WOOD IS ABLE TO RESIST BENDING FORCES
BETTER THAN MATERIALS SUCH AS STONE, WHICH FRACTURE
EASILY. FOR THIS REASON, WOOD HAS BEEN
FAVORED FOR CENTURIES AS A GOOD MATERIAL
TO SPAN THE LIVING SPACE AND
SUPPORT THE WEIGHT OF THE ROOF
AND SNOW.

BENDING FORCE

MANDAN HOUSE, AMERICAN NORTHERN
PLAINS

PREHISTORIC PITHOUSE
WITH POLE ROOF

HOUSE FRAME
PENNSYLVANIA
(CA. 1700)

THE SAME FRAMING SYSTEM USED IN
THE PREHISTORIC PITHOUSE ABOVE IS
THE MOST COMMON ROOF CONSTRUCTION
TECHNIQUE USED TODAY. IT CONSISTS
OF RAFTERS SPANNING FROM THE
WALL SILL OR BEAM TO THE RIDGE.
MODERN FRAMING USUALLY INCLUDES
A BOARD AT THE RIDGE.

IN AREAS WHERE HEAVY TIMBER WAS NOT AVAILABLE FOR USE AS STRAIGHT ROOF BEAMS THE VAULT AROSE AS A SUBSTITUTE. BY SIMPLY SECURING ONE END OF A SAPLING, BENDING IT, AND SECURING THE OTHER END ONE CAN CREATE AN ARCH. A SERIES OF THESE FORMS A VAULT. IT IS NO SURPRISE THAT THIS IS, PERHAPS, THE MOST WIDESPREAD ROOF FORM.

VAULTED HOUSE
CAREENING BAY, AUSTRALIA

ALTERNATIVE MATERIALS, SUCH AS STONE, CLAY, OR BRICK, ARE STRONG WHEN BEING COMPRESSED BUT WEAK WHEN BEING BENT. A HORIZONTAL ROOF BEAM EXPERIENCES BENDING, BUT IN A VAULT OR DOME ALL THE ELEMENTS ARE UNDER COMPRESSION, SO IT IS A FORM THAT IS PARTICULARLY SUITED TO THOSE MATERIALS.

BARREL VAULTED HOUSES
GREECE

THIS STRUCTURE, CALLED A "CASELLA," HAS AN INNER CORBELED STONE DOME COVERED WITH EARTH AND AN OUTER STONE SURFACE.

"CASELLA"; APULIA, ITALY

CONICAL DOMED ROOF OF HAND-MOLDED CLAY
NORTHERN CAMEROON

MUD BRICK SAIL VAULTS BUILT ON RUBBLE STONE WALLS

CARAVANSARAI; QUM, IRAN

TRUSSES

IN A SIMPLE GABLE ROOF, THE DOWNWARD FORCES FROM THE WEIGHT OF THE ROOFING AND ANY SNOW WILL CAUSE BENDING IN THE RAFTERS AND EXERT AN OUTWARD FORCE AT THE BASE OF THE ROOF.

TRUSSES GIVE THE RAFTERS ADDITIONAL BRACING AND TIE THE BASE OF THE ROOF TOGETHER SO THAT IT DOESN'T SPREAD AND COLLAPSE.

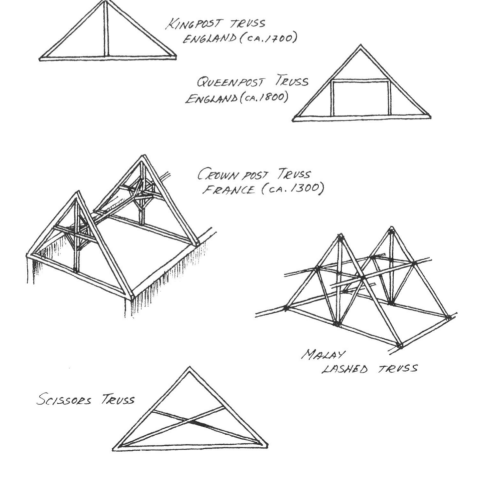

KINGPOST TRUSS
ENGLAND (CA. 1700)

QUEENPOST TRUSS
ENGLAND (CA. 1800)

CROWN POST TRUSS
FRANCE (CA. 1300)

MALAY LASHED TRUSS

SCISSORS TRUSS

Roofing Materials

Vegetal Roofs:

Roof of palm leaves
laid shingle style

Johore, Malaysia

Kirdi hut with roof
of piled grass

Multi-layer, built-up
thatch roof
Sudan

Thatched cottage
France (ca. 1885)

Thatched roof
with a partial hip on
a gable, called a
Jerkin head

Hampshire, England

THATCH:

VIEW OF UNDERSIDE OF REED AND
THATCH ROOF WITH BAMBOO
RAFTERS

KATSURA, JAPAN
(CA. 1630)

BAMBOO
REED
THATCH

SECTION THROUGH
BAMBOO SUPPORTED
THATCH ROOF (JAPAN)

BAMBOO

STEEP ROOFS DIVERT
HEAVY, TROPICAL RAINS

GRASS THATCH HUTS
INSIDE A STONE ENCLOSURE
(MARQUESAS ISLANDS)

ROCK
FOUNDATION

SECTION THROUGH ROOF
SHOWING OVERLAP ON
STONE WALL

ROPE STITCHING TO PREVENT WIND FROM
LIFTING THE THATCH
SUSSEX, ENGLAND
(CA. 1699)

HAT-LIKE CAPS ON
THATCHED ROOFS GIVE
ACCESS TO GRANARIES.

DORMER WINDOWS IN A
THATCHED ROOF

KENT, ENGLAND

STONE ROOFS

SLATE ROOF
AND CHIMNEY

STONE ROOF AND WALL
BORGONE, ITALY

DETAIL OF INTERLOCKING
SLATES AT THE ROOF RIDGE

PEÑALBA DE SANTIAGO,
SPAIN

SLATE ROOF
WITH TERRA-COTTA
TILE TO SEAL THE RIDGE

CHAMONIX, FRANCE

SLATE ROOF WITH
ROCKS TO PREVENT
WIND DAMAGE

SWITZERLAND

SOME CUT SLATE
PATTERNS

SQUARED

BEVELED

DIAMOND

OUTER ROOF

EARTH

THE TRULLO STRUCTURES
OF APULIA HAVE AN INNER
STONE VAULT AND AN OUTER
ROOF OF STONES THAT ARE SLIGHTLY
TILTED TO DIVERT WATER.

APULIA, ITALY

PANTILE ROOF
NETHERLANDS (17ᵗʰ CENTURY)

MISSION TILE ROOF
MEXICO

MISSION
TILE

MEXICO (CA. 1800)

DETAIL OF
CEMENTED JOINT AT
THE RIDGE

TILED GABLE AND SHED ROOFS
PROVENCE, FRANCE

JAPANESE YEDO TILE

TILES AT THE
EAVES HAVE
AN ORNAMENTAL
DESIGN.

TILED HOUSE, HAKODATE,
JAPAN (CA. 1880)

VAULTED ROOF UNDER
CONSTRUCTION; NOTE THE
RECTANGULAR BRICK-LIKE
TILE BLOCKS.

TUNISIA

Wooden Roofs

In areas where tree bark can be harvested in large sheets, it is often used as a roofing material. In this example, poles secure the bark.

BARK COVERED HUT
NEW ENGLAND INDIANS
(CA. 1600)

Thick slabs of bark can also be used like mission tiles (see page 112).

Logs themselves have sometimes been used for roofing, as in the scoop-log roof (right), or the split log roof (left).

SCOOP-LOG
ROOF

SPLIT LOG ROOF
HELSINKI, FINLAND

ROOF OF
HAND-SPLIT SHAKES
NORTH CAROLINA
(CA. 1750)

MAUL

SHAKES ARE
MADE BY SPLITTING
A LOG WITH A FROE
AND A MAUL.

SHAKE

FROE

ROOF OF SHAPED BOARDS
HORIUJI, JAPAN

BOARD ROOF, OR
"HISASHI"

KYOTO, JAPAN

LOG HOUSE WITH SHINGLE ROOF
CZECHOSLOVAKIA (1903)

FOR WEATHER PROTECTION, THE NEXT BEST THING TO DIGGING INTO THE EARTH IS TO PILE EARTH ON TOP.

SOD-ROOFED CABIN
COPENHAGEN, DENMARK

WHEN PROPERLY PACKED AND FINISHED, AND KEPT FREE OF STANDING WATER, A ROOF MADE FROM MUD CAN BE IMPERVIOUS TO RAIN AND CAN INSULATE THE DWELLING.

HERRINGBONE PATTERN OF CEILING BOARDS SUPPORTING AN ADOBE ROOF.

SAN ANTONIO, TEXAS (CA. 1860)

ADOBE ROOF

ADOBE

GRASS AND TWIGS

LOG BEAM

TAOS, NEW MEXICO (CA. 1600)

STICK AND POLE STRUCTURAL SYSTEM SUPPORTING A ROOF OF CALICHE, A SOIL WITH A HIGH LIME CONTENT.

CASA GRANDE, ARIZONA (CA. 1250)

WHITEWASH
MUD
TWIG MAT
LOG BEAM

ROOF SYSTEM
PAKISTAN

NEBRASKA SODDIE (CA. 1886)

THE BUILDERS OF THE SOD HOUSES OF THE PLAINS STATES USED SOD TO CONSTRUCT THE WALLS AND ALSO AS A COVERING FOR THE WOOD ROOF.

THE CUBITERMES TERMITES
USE SOIL PARTICLES CEMENTED
WITH EXCREMENT TO BUILD THEIR
LARGE, MUSHROOM-SHAPED COLONIES.
THE DOMED ROOF ACTS LIKE
AN UMBRELLA TO DIVERT
THE HEAVY TROP-
ICAL RAINS.

CUBITERMES COLONY

ALASKAN ESKIMO WINTER
HOUSE WITH EARTH
COVERING

FRONT ELEVATION

ONLY THE TWO SMALL
GABLE ENDS OF THIS EARTH-
COVERED HOUSE ARE EXPOSED
TO THE WEATHER.

EARTH

PLAN

GREECE (1876)

MANY OF THE OLD BUILDINGS
IN ICELAND HAVE THEIR WALLS
PROTECTED FROM THE COLD BY
LARGE MASSES OF EARTH. BLOCKS
OF TURF ARE COURSED IN A
HERRINGBONE PATTERN AND
ALSO CARRIED UP OVER
THE ROOF.

OLD CHURCH
ICELAND

CONTEMPORARY
EARTH-SHELTERED
HOUSE
LYME, NEW HAMPSHIRE

OTHER ROOFING MATERIALS:

SKINS:

INUIT "TUPIQ"
THE INUIT SUMMER DWELLING,
OR "TUPIQ," IS MADE FROM SEAL-
SKINS STRETCHED OVER A WOODEN
FRAME AND HELD SECURE BY GUY
ROPES AND ROCKS AROUND THE
PERIMETER.

PLAINS INDIAN TEPEE
A SKIN MEMBRANE IS
ATTACHED TO BOTH THE
INSIDE AND THE OUTSIDE
OF THE POLES.

FABRIC:

MOOR TENT FROM MAURITANIA
FABRIC MADE OF GOAT HAIR IS STRETCHED
OVER A FEW POLES AND STAKED WITH
THE OPENING DOWNWIND.

YURT FROM KIRGHIZISTAN
MULTI-LAYER GOAT HAIR FABRIC IS
TIED OVER A WOODEN FRAME.

METAL:

RAISED,
CLAD
JOINT

FACIA

TIN ROOF
ELKHORN, MONTANA (CA. 1890)
IT WENT UP QUICKLY BUT
WAS A POOR INSULATOR.

COPPER CLAD ROOF
NIKKO, JAPAN
(CA. 1500)
IT WEATHERS WELL AND
TAKES ON A NICE PATINA.

OTHER:

DULLES AIRPORT, VIRGINIA
CABLE-SUPPORTED CONCRETE ROOF

AIR-SUPPORTED TENNIS COURT
ENCLOSURE OF SYNTHETIC
FABRIC, BOSTON

THE WALL

As the wall became a separate structure from the roof it also took on separate functions. Beyond insulating the house, the roof is built to keep out rain, snow, and sun, while the primitive wall deals with wind, animals, and neighbors.

In its simplest form, the wall is a light vegetal membrane that offers privacy, shade, and protection from wind and rain.

BAMBOO AND REED WALL
FIJI ISLANDS

AÏR-TUAREG TENT
WITH MOVABLE WALLS OF
WOVEN STRAW

Woven walls offer shade and rain protection but allow some air flow, which is essential in humid climates.

HERRINGBONE WEAVE

UPPER VOLTA

WALL OF SAPLINGS LAID BETWEEN PAIRS OF PERIMETER POSTS

POKOT DWELLING
KENYA

STILT HOUSE
WITH SPLIT
BAMBOO
WALLS

ROLL-DOWN
WOVEN WALL
PANELS

GILBERT
ISLANDS

SOUTH DAHOMEY

THE LOG WALL

THE INSULATING PROPERTIES OF SOLID WOOD AND THE PREVALENCE OF FORESTS IN COOLER CLIMATES PROMOTE LOG WALL CONSTRUCTION IN THOSE AREAS.

PLAN OF A "SRUB"

RUSSIA HAS SOME OF THE EARLIEST LOG STRUCTURES. THEY ARE BASED ON A UNIT CALLED A "SRUB," A SIMPLE SQUARE FORMED BY FOUR TREE TRUNKS. THE NOREGIANS EXTENDED THE SIDES BY JOINING SEVERAL LOGS END-TO-END.

CROSS SECTIONS OF COMMON LOG TREATMENTS:

 RUSSIAN (UNTRIMMED)

 NORWEGIAN (2 SIDES SQUARED)

 ALPINE (4 SIDES SQUARED)

YUKAGHIR LOG HOUSE WITH A SOD ROOF SIBERIA

LOG CABIN WITH CHINKING TO SEAL THE GAP BETWEEN THE LOGS.

INDIANA (CA. 1850)

YAKUT VERTICAL LOG WALL WITH COVERING OF MUD

SIBERIA

LOG STOREHOUSE ALVROS, SWEDEN (CA. 1753)

THE MORE PRIMITIVE LOG
JOINTS ARE MADE BY
CUTTING A SMALL SADDLE
OUT OF THE TOP AND
BOTTOM OF
EACH LOG.

V-NOTCH

SADDLE JOINT

SHAPING THE LOG SO
THAT IT HAS A PEAKED UPPER
SURFACE AND CUTTING V-NOTCHES
IN THE BOTTOM CREATES A
JOINT THAT WILL REDUCE ROT,
BECAUSE IT DOES NOT
TRAP WATER.

HEWN LOGS
WITH A
SADDLE
NOTCH

THIS JOINT COMBINES THE
SIMPLICITY OF THE SADDLE JOINT WITH
THE DRAINING ADVANTAGE OF
THE V-NOTCH.

DOUBLE-DEN OR
DOUBLE-PEN
LOG HOUSE

(CENTER HALL
GAVE ADDED
VENTILATION)

PLAN

WILSON, ARKANSAS

AS TIMBER-SHAPING TECHNOL-
OGY IMPROVED, TIGHTER AND MORE
COMPLEX JOINTS WERE USED.

V-NOTCH

SQUARE
NOTCH

DIAMOND

DOVETAIL

DOUBLE NOTCH

INDENTED V-NOTCH

Wood Walls

ADVANCES IN WOOD SAWING AND MILLING TECHNOLOGY GREATLY REFINED THE WOOD FRAMING SYSTEMS AND ALSO BROUGHT ABOUT THE EXTENSIVE USE OF SAWN BOARDS AS A SIDING MATERIAL. A VARIETY OF TYPES AROSE IN AN EFFORT TO CREATE A TIGHT WALL WITH ROT-RESISTANT JOINTS.

EDGE LAP

CLAPBOARDS

BEVELED

RABBETED OR SHIPLAP

BOARD AND BATTEN:
WITH WOOD STRIPS,

WITH BAMBOO

THE SIDING AND ROOFIN'S OF MANY OLD BARNS HAD SLIGHTLY OPEN JOINTS TO LET THE BARN BREATHE. IN THE RAIN, THE WOOD SWELLED AND CLOSED THE GAP.

NEW HAMPSHIRE FARMHOUSE WITH AN ATTACHED SHED (CA. 1840)

HORIZONTAL BOARDS WITH RECESSED BATTENS — BY FRANK LLOYD WRIGHT

FARMHOUSE WALL BERN, SWITZERLAND

WATTLE AND DAUB

THE USE OF MUD PLASTER (DAUB) OVER A MATRIX OF WOOD, REED, OR BAMBOO STRIPS (WATTLE) TO BUILD WALLS ACTUALLY PRE-DATES THE EGYPTIAN CULTURE.

HUNGARIAN PEASANT HOUSE

WATTLE AND DAUB WALL

THE EARLIEST FORM OF MUD-PLASTERED WALL CONSTRUCTION WAS PROBABLY JACAL (MUD OVER VERTICAL PIECES PLANTED IN THE GROUND).

JACAL WALL, KEET SEEL, NAVAHO NATIONAL MONUMENT, ARIZONA

HORIZONTAL WOOD STRIPS LASHED TO POSTS AND THEN PLASTERED WITH MUD THAT HAS BEEN MIXED WITH STRAW TO HOLD IT TOGETHER

VENEZUELA

THE BAMBOO MESH IN THIS WALL HAS BEEN LEFT UNPLASTERED IN ONE SECTION TO LEAVE A WINDOW WITH A GRILLE.

JAPAN

A MORE ADVANCED USE OF THE WATTLE AND DAUB IS IN HALF-TIMBER CONSTRUCTION. THE WATTLE IS FRAMED INTO THE TIMBER STRUCTURE, THEN PLASTERED, LEAVING THE TIMBERS EXPOSED.

ENGLAND

IN OTHER HALF-TIMBER CONSTRUCTION, MASONRY FILLS IN THE WALL AREA BETWEEN THE TIMBERS.

BRICK INFILLED HALF-TIMBER HOUSE NEWGATE, YORK ENGLAND (CA. 1380)

A VERY COMMON, PRIMITIVE TYPE OF WALL IS THAT OF HAND-FORMED MUD COURSES.

NORTHERN IVORY COAST

COB (MUD MIXED WITH STRAW FOR ADDED STRENGTH) WAS A FAVORITE BUILDING MATERIAL IN MANY PARTS OF ENGLAND.

STONE ENDED COB HOUSE DEVON, ENGLAND

WALLS OF TABBY, A MIXTURE OF LIME, SAND, WATER, AND AGGREGATE (BROKEN SHELLS), ARE COMMON IN OLDER HOMES IN THE SOUTHERN U.S. THE WALLS WERE FORMED BY POURING THE TABBY BETWEEN FORM BOARDS (SEE PAGE 103).

ST. AUGUSTINE, FLORIDA

SOME WASPS BUILD TUBULAR NESTS BY FASHIONING SMALL MUD CYLINDERS AND THEN LAYERING THEM TO CREATE THE ARCHED SHAPE OF THE NEST.

WASP'S NEST

FOR OVER 8,000 YEARS, CULTURES THE WORLD OVER HAVE BUILT WITH MUD BRICKS. THE SHAPING OF THE BRICKS WAS ORIGINALLY DONE BY HAND AND LATER WITH MOLDS. DURABILITY WAS INCREASED BY FIRING THEM.

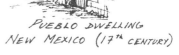

BRICK AND MOLD
MALI

AFTER THE ARRIVAL OF THE SPANISH IN AMERICA THE PUEBLO INDIANS BEGAN BUILDING WITH ADOBE BRICKS RATHER THAN WITH HAND-SHAPED OR PUDDLED ADOBE.

PUEBLO DWELLING
NEW MEXICO (17TH CENTURY)

MUD BRICK WALL
AND PANTILE ROOF
VENEZUELA

BECAUSE OF THEIR SQUARE AND REGULAR SHAPE, BRICKS ARE OFTEN USED IN CONJUNCTION WITH STONE TO MAKE SOLID, SQUARE CORNERS, DOOR AND WINDOW JAMBS, FLAT OR ARCHED LINTELS, SILLS, AND CHIMNEYS.

FLINT COBBLE AND BRICK HOUSE
NORFOLK, ENGLAND

TUMBLED BRICKWORK SERVES AS BOTH A STRENGTHENING AND A DECORATIVE ELEMENT.

PROVINCE DU NORD, FRANCE

BRICK WALL WITH CUT STONE QUOINS GIVING ADDED SOLIDITY AT THE DOORWAY

VAL D'OISE, FRANCE

DECORATIVE WALL TREATMENTS COMBINING AREAS OF STONE AND BRICK

BRAY, FRANCE

NORMANDY, FRANCE

A COMMON PRACTICE IS TO REINFORCE THE CORNERS OF BRICK STRUCTURES WITH LARGE, CUT STONE QUOINS.

BRICK, STONE, AND THATCH HOUSE ; TIDPIT HAMPSHIRE, ENGLAND

STONE

As well as being an efficient way to enclose space (see page 27), the stone beehive hut does not require the complex fashioning of corners in stone.

STONE AGE BEEHIVE HUT, IRELAND

MASSIVE (NOTE SCALE FIGURE) AND INTRICATELY SHAPED AND FITTED STONES

SACSAHUAMAN, A STONE AGE INDIAN FORTRESS; CUZCO, PERU

Where a variety of stone is available, it often inspires decorative patterns.

CHACO CANYON, NEW MEXICO (CA. 1100)

SLATE AND BOULDERS NORTHERN ENGLAND

WALLS OF GREEN SLATE WITH QUOINS AND LINTELS OF SLATE PLACED ON EDGE

ELTERWATER CUMBRIA, ENGLAND

THE CORNICE, WINDOW JAMBS,
AND TRIANGULAR ARCH ARE
OF CUT STONE, WHILE THE
WALL IS OF SLATE WITH
BANDS OF RUBBLE STONE.

FRANCE

STONE SEGMENTAL ARCH
PENNSYLVANIA (18ᵗʰ CENTURY)

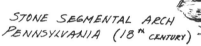

EXTENDED WOOD LINTEL
FOR ADDED TENSILE STRENGTH

PUEBLO BONITO (CA. 1050)

CUT STONE LINTEL,
OR FLAT ARCH

ENGLAND (CA. 1618)

SQUARED BLOCKS,
CORNICEWORK, AND
SEMICIRCULAR
ARCHES – ALL
CUT FROM
LOCAL SANDSTONE.

TIGHT-FITTING
POLYGONAL
STONEWORK

HOT SPRINGS, SOUTH DAKOTA (CA. 1891)   KYOTO, JAPAN (CA. 1600)

IN EASTERN PORTUGAL SOME HOUSES HAVE A STONE WALL SYSTEM CONSISTING OF HUGE GRANITE SLABS AS MUCH AS TWELVE INCHES THICK SURROUNDED AND HELD IN PLACE BY SMALLER STONES.

GRANITE SLABS ARE ALSO USED FOR ROOFING AND PAVING.

WYTHES   BINDING STONE

TO MAKE A THICK, SOLID STONE WALL, SEVERAL TIERS, OR WYTHES, OF STONE ARE BUILT AND TIED TOGETHER AT INTERVALS WITH BINDING STONES. SOMETIMES THESE STONES PROTRUDE AND ARE USED AS SHELVES OR STAIRS.

THE INCA INDIANS OF PERU WERE ACCOMPLISHED STONE MASONS AND DEVELOPED THE TECHNIQUE OF USING COPPER CRAMPS TO HOLD STONES TOGETHER. THE METHOD THEY USED MAY HAVE BEEN TO POUR MOLTEN COPPER INTO PREPARED HOLES IN THE STONES.

COPPER CRAMP

ANOTHER TECHNIQUE EMPLOYED BY THE INCAS WAS TO USE LONG STONES PROTRUDING FROM THE WALLS AS SUPPORTS FOR THE FLOOR JOISTS AND ROOF RAFTERS.

PERUVIAN ANDES 15th CENTURY

HYBRIDS:

A TRADEMARK OF INDIGENOUS ARCHITECTURE IS THE USE OF A VARIETY OF MATERIALS IN WAYS THAT TAKE BEST ADVANTAGE OF THEIR PARTICULAR PROPERTIES.

THE BUILDERS OF THIS PRIMITIVE, DECAYING HOUSE BUILT A SOLID FOUNDATION OF STONE, A LIGHT FRAME OF WOOD, A WATERPROOF ROOF OF THATCH, AND AN UPPER, WEATHERTIGHT WALL OF WATTLE AND DAUB.

THIS NORWEGIAN HOUSE HAS A FIRM STONE FOUN- DATION, A SOLID FIRST- FLOOR BARN AND STORAGE AREA OF LOGS, AN UPPER LIVING AREA WITH TIMBER FRAMING AND LIGHT PLANK WALLS, AND AN INSULATING ROOF OF SOD OVER BARK.

A BARN IN HAGI, JAPAN WITH A MASSIVE STONE BASE, LOWER AND GABLE WALLS OF BOARDS OVER A TIMBER FRAME, OPEN-SLATTED WALL IN LOFT FOR VENTILATION, AND A TILE ROOF

AN OLD SWISS
FARMHOUSE WITH LOWER
WALLS OF STONE; OVER
THAT, A TIMBER FRAME
WITH WATTLE AND
DAUB INFILL, AND
A TILE ROOF
WITH DEEP
OVERHANGS

BERNESE FARMHOUSE
SWITZERLAND

HAGI, JAPAN

A GARDEN WALL WITH A
COMBINATION OF STONE, EDGE-
LAPPED BOARDS WITH EXTERIOR
BATTENS, PLASTER OVER BAMBOO,
AND TILE

POLE FRAME
WITH ROCK INFILL
AND PANTILE ROOF

GREECE

COTTAGE WITH STONE
BASE, END WALLS, AND
SEMICIRCULAR ARCHES,
UPPER WALL OF HALF-
TIMBER CONSTRUCTION,
AND ROOF OF
SHINGLES

JOSSELIN, FRANCE

THE EARLY SETTLERS IN THE AMERICAN MID-WEST HAD FEW BUILD-ING MATERIALS AVAILABLE SO THEY OFTEN USED BLOCKS OF SOD TO CONSTRUCT WALLS AND TO COVER THE ROOF.

SOD HOUSE; NEBRASKA (19ᵗʰ CENTURY)

ANOTHER SIMPLE, EFFECTIVE, AND INEX-PENSIVE SYSTEM IS THE STOVEWOOD WALL. IN WOODPILE FASHION THE LOGS ARE STACKED AND MORTARED LIKE STONE-WORK. NOTE THE LOG QUOINS THAT REINFORCE THE CORNER.

STOVEWOOD WALL; CANADA

IN THE LATE NINETEENTH AND EARLY TWENTIETH CENTURIES TIN WAS USE EXTENSIVELY AS A CHEAP, WEATHER-RESISTANT COVERING FOR BARNS AND HOMES.

TIN SHINGLES AND PANELS MAINE

CEDAR SHINGLES HAVE BEEN WIDELY USED FOR CENTURIES AS BOTH A ROOF AND A WALL MATERIAL BECAUSE OF THEIR EXCELLENT WEATHER-RESISTANT QUALITIES.

SHINGLED HOUSE; HINGHAM, MASSACHUSETTS (1720)

BARN WITH WALLS
MADE OF BALES OF
HAY STAKED TOGETHER
AND ROOF MADE
OF STRAW

NEBRASKA (CA. 1910)

ENGLISH WALL TILES ARE LAPPED
LIKE SHINGLES, LEAVING
THE NAILS AND JOINTS
PROTECTED.

JAPANESE
FLAT TILES
ARE NAILED AT THE
CORNERS AND THEN THE
JOINTS ARE PLASTERED.

THE
BOTTLE
WALL

BOTTLES ARE LAID IN
MORTAR. THEY ADMIT
A BEAUTIFUL LIGHT
BUT INSULATE POORLY.

IN A SLIP-
FORMED STONE
WALL ROCKS ARE
PLACED BETWEEN
THE FORM BOARDS
AND CONCRETE IS
POURED. LATER,
THE FORM IS
SLIPPED UP TO HOLD
THE NEXT COURSE.

FORM BOARD

FORM
BRACE

IN MANY AREAS
SUBSTANTIAL HEATING CAN
BE SUPPLIED BY THE USE OF
GLASS ON THE SOUTH WALLS
TO TRAP SOLAR HEAT
INSIDE THE HOUSE.

CONTEMPORARY PASSIVE SOLAR
HOUSE WITH ATTACHED GREENHOUSE
NEW LONDON, NEW HAMPSHIRE

THE FLOOR

NEOLITHIC PIT HOUSE

THE SIMPLEST AND MOST COMMON FLOOR SURFACES FOUND IN PRIMITIVE DWELLINGS ARE OF PACKED EARTH AND ARE SOMETIMES COVERED WITH LEAVES, STRAW, SKINS, OR WOVEN MATS.

A FLOOR OF POURED MORTAR AND AGGREGATE MIXTURES, SUCH AS TABBY, GIVES A SURFACE THAT IS MORE DURABLE, CLEANER, AND DRIER. WHEN WORN, A NEW LAYER IS POURED ON TOP.

TABBY (2 IN.)

SHELLSTONE BASE (3 IN.)

ST. AUGUSTINE, FLORIDA (CA. 1700)

FLAT STONES ARE USED ALL OVER THE WORLD TO CREATE VERY DURABLE FLOORS AND PAVEMENTS.

APULIA, ITALY (CA. 1600)

EARLY WOOD FLOORS WERE OF RIVED BOARDS RESTING ON LOG JOISTS THAT HAD BEEN MADE FLAT ON THE UPPER SIDE WITH AN ADZE OR A BROADAXE. THE BOARDS WERE TRIMMED OR SHIMMED AT THE JOIST TO KEEP THE FLOOR LEVEL.

RIVED BOARD

LOG JOIST

TONGUE AND GROOVE

SPLINE

SPLINED AND TONGUE-AND-GROOVE BOARDS TIE THE FLOOR TOGETHER FOR GREATER STRENGTH AND FOR LESS WARPING.

STRAW TATAMI MAT (176 cm × 88 cm)

IN JAPAN, THE FLOOR MATERIAL DEFINES THE NATURE OF THE VARIOUS SPACES: EARTH OR STONE IN THE BARN AND ENTRANCE, WOOD IN THE KITCHEN AND WALKWAYS, AND TATAMI MATS IN THE LIVING AREAS. ROOM SIZES, AND SOMETIMES LAND AREAS, ARE MEASURED BY THE NUMBER OF TATAMI MATS HAVING AN EQUIVALENT AREA — FOR EXAMPLE, A SIX-MAT ROOM ACCOMODATES SIX TATAMI MATS.

LIVING (TATAMIS)   KITCHEN (WOOD)   ENTRY   (STONE)

SECTION THROUGH A TRADITIONAL JAPANESE HOUSE

The Chimney

MANY PRIMITIVE DWELLINGS HAVE NO OUTLET SPECIFICALLY FOR THE SMOKE FROM THE FIRE. IN THE COMMUNAL HOUSES OF THE WAURA INDIANS, THE SMOKE INSIDE HELPS TO KEEP PESTS OUT, AND IT ALSO PROTECTS THE THATCH FROM INSECTS AS IT FILTERS OUT.

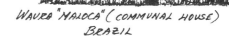

WAURA "MALOCA" (COMMUNAL HOUSE) BRAZIL

PAN-P'O DWELLING, CHINA (4000 B.C.) NOTE THE SMOKE HOLE AT THE PEAK OF THE EARTH-COVERED ROOF.

STONE SLAB USED AS A RAIN HOOD OVER THE SMOKE HOLE (ZUNI PUEBLO, NEW MEXICO)

IN MANY PRIMITIVE DWELLINGS AN OPENING IN THE ROOF ACTS AS THE ENTRANCE, THE SOURCE OF LIGHT, AND THE SMOKE HOLE.

HOUSE IN ANATOLIA, TURKEY (6000 B.C.)

STONE SLAB HOOD OVER SMOKE HOLE ST. AUGUSTINE, FLORIDA (CA. 1765)

SHORT CHIMNEY MADE FROM OLD CLAY POTS ZUNI PUEBLO, NEW MEXICO

ADOBE FIRE-PLACE AND CHIM-NEY NEW MEXICO (CA. 1850)

DURING THE LAST SEVERAL CENTURIES THE FIREPLACE AND THE ENCLOSED CHIM-NEY HAVE REPLACED THE FIRE PIT AND THE SMOKE HOLE IN MOST AREAS.

THE FIREPLACE ITSELF IS ALWAYS MADE OF SOME MINERAL MATERIAL, BUT CHIMNEYS HAVE BEEN BUILT WITH A VARIETY OF MATERIALS.

THE LOG CHIMNEY'S INTERIOR IS PLASTERED WITH MORTAR TO PROTECT IT FROM THE HEAT OF THE FIRE.

LOG CHIMNEY
INDIANA (CA. 1850)

THIS LARGE WOODEN CHIMNEY FORMS A FUNNEL-SHAPED HOOD OVER A WALK-IN STONE FIREPLACE.

SWITZERLAND

HOOD

CELLAR

(SECTION THROUGH HOUSE)

VIRGINIA (18th CENTURY)

THIS BRICK CHIMNEY IS SET OUT FROM THE WALL TO REDUCE THE FIRE HAZARD AND THE HEAT INPUT DURING SUMMER.

THIS MASSIVE CHIMNEY SERVES A LARGE FIRST-FLOOR AND A SMALL UPSTAIRS FIREPLACE PLUS A BAKE OVEN.

VIRGINIA (18th CENTURY)

COMBINED SMOKEHOUSE
AND SPRINGHOUSE WITH
A STAIRWAY BUILT INTO
THE CHIMNEY

CHESTER COUNTY
PENNSYLVANIA

LIKE CURVED WALLS (SEE PAGE 125),
ROUND CHIMNEYS SAVE THE DIFFICULT
TASK OF MAKING CORNERS WHEN WORKING
WITH FLAT STONES, SUCH AS SLATE.

PLASTERED,
ROUND, STONE
CHIMNEY WITH
SLATE RAIN SHIELD
(NORTHERN ENGLAND)

SHINGLED CHIMNEY
WITH RAIN HOOD (ALPS)

THIS CHIMNEY IS
INTEGRATED WITH THE
STUCCOED STONEWORK
OF THE HOUSE.

CHESTER COUNTY
PENNSYLVANIA

A SECTION TAKEN THROUGH THE
VAULTED HALLWAY OF THIS HOUSE SHOWS
HOW THE TWO FIREPLACE FLUES ARE
JOINED IN ONE CHIMNEY.

ASH LAWN, VIRGINIA
(DESIGNED BY THOMAS JEFFERSON)

THE SIMPLEST DOORWAYS ARE SIMPLY HOLES IN THE WALL, LIKE THIS PREHISTORIC DOOR OPENING CARVED FROM A STONE SLAB.

MALTA

USING TAPERED JAMBS CAN REDUCE THE SIZE OF THE STONE LINTEL AND CAN ALSO MAKE THE OPENING APPEAR TALLER

MYCENAE, GREECE (1325 B.C.)

THE SHAPES OF THE OPENINGS BELOW ALLOW PEOPLE TO PUT THEIR HANDS ON THE SIDE AND SWING THEIR LEGS OVER THE HIGH THRESHOLD AND ALSO PERMIT SOMEONE TO ENTER WHILE CARRYING A WIDE LOAD.

MESAKIN DWELLING,

SUDAN

PUEBLO BONITO, NEW MEXICO (11th CENTURY)

NARROW, RECESSED DOORS REDUCE THE AMOUNT OF SUNLIGHT ENTERING AND HEATING THE INTERIOR.

MYKONOS, GREECE

MANY AFRICAN DWELLINGS HAVE SMALL RAISED OPENINGS THAT MINIMIZE THE PASSAGE OF THE SUN'S HEAT AND ALSO DETER ANIMALS FROM CRAWLING IN.

NORTHERN CAMEROON

DOORS FOR SECURITY

MASSIVE WOOD DOOR
WITH HEAVY, METAL REIN-
FORCING PLATES AND
HINGES

TOWER OF LONDON
(CA. 1097)

AT THE ENTRANCE TO ITS NEST IN A
DRY BANK THE TRAP-DOOR SPIDER
CONSTRUCTS A SILK-HINGED DOOR
BY CEMENTING SOIL PARTICLES.
IT CLOSES UNDER ITS OWN
WEIGHT TO NEATLY COVER THE
NEST'S OPENING.

A PAIR OF HEAVY WOOD
DOORS ("PORTON") USED TO CLOSE
OFF THE PLAZA ("ZAGUAN") OF A
HACIENDA AND CONTAINING A
SMALLER, INSET DOOR, WHICH IS
USED MORE OFTEN

THE SMALL (4 FEET HIGH) MOTHER-IN-LAW
DOOR GIVES ACCESS TO AND FROM BOATS
IN THE CANALS.

AMSTERDAM

THE ANCIENT
PRACTICE OF ENTERING THE
HOUSE VIA A FULLY ENCLOSED
COURTYARD HAS REMAINED
POPULAR FOR CENTURIES
FOR REASONS OF SECURITY
AND PRIVACY.

CHARLESTON
SOUTH CAROLINA (19th CENTURY)

DOORWAY WITH PROTECTIVE DECORATIVE GRILLE IN THE TRANSOM OPENING, WHICH PERMITS VENTILATION.

MORELOS, MEXICO

SLIDING, SLATTED FRAME IN THE TRANSOM CAN BE LEFT OPEN OR CLOSED.

JAPAN

THE TRADITIONAL DOOR IN JAPAN IS A SLIDING PANEL. THE EXTERIOR ONES, OR SHOJIS, ARE OF WOOD COVERED WITH RICE PAPER, WHILE THE INTERIOR ONES, OR FUSUMAS, ARE OF WOOD COVERED WITH A SOLID MATERIAL OR CLOTH. ABOVE THE FUSUMA IS OFTEN AN OPEN SPACE, OR RAMMA (USUALLY HAVING A DECORATIVE GRILLEWORK), FOR VENTILATION.

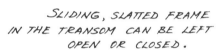

RAMA

FUSUMA

LOUVERED DOORS GIVE PRIVACY WHILE ALLOWING GOOD VENTILATION, AND THE TRANSOM WINDOW LETS IN LIGHT AND/OR FRESH AIR.

BERMUDA

138

DOORWAY WITH
WOOD LATTICE SCREEN IN
BOTH THE DOORS AND THE
TRANSOM FOR LIGHT
AND VENTILATION

VENEZUELA

DUTCH DOOR WITH BOTTOM CLOSED
TO KEEP ANIMALS OUT AND CHILDREN
IN AND WITH TOP OPEN FOR
LIGHT AND AIR

PENNSYLVANIA

SOLID LOWER
DOOR AND BI-FOLD
UPPER DOORS FOR A
DUTCH DOOR EFFECT,
PLUS A TRANSOM
WINDOW

GREECE

GRILLES ALLOW AIR AND VIEW THROUGH
THE DOORS, WHICH ENCLOSE
THE "ZAGUAN."

CALIFORNIA

THE SMALL GLASS
INSERTS IN THESE SHOJIS
CAN BE SLID OPEN FOR VEN-
TILATION OR CAN BE COVERED
BY SMALL SLIDING PANELS OF
TRANSLUCENT RICE PAPER FOR
PRIVACY. AS WINDOWS THEY
OFFER A NICE VIEW FOR
PEOPLE SEATED ON THE FLOOR.

JAPAN

LINTEL

HARR

SLAB DOOR

THIS DOOR, MADE FROM A LARGE SLAB OF WOOD, HAS TWO PROJECTING LOBES, OR HARRS, WHICH ROTATE IN HOLES IN THE LINTEL AND THRESH-OLD. THESE HARR-HUNG, OR PINTLE, DOORS WERE USED IN THE NEAR EAST MORE THAN 6,000 YEARS AGO.

ZAMBIA

LINTEL, OR "KAMOI," WITH ROUTED TRACKS FOR THE FUSUMAS

JAPAN

CLOTH USED FOR PRIVACY AND SHADING IN DOORWAY

APULIA, ITALY

DOORWAY WITH RAIN HOOD

BUCKS COUNTY PENNSYLVANIA (19ᵗʰ CENTURY)

PLAN OF DOORWAY SHOWING HOW THE DOUBLE DOORS FOLD AWAY INTO THE JAMBS

VISCHE, ITALY (15ᵗʰ CENTURY)

THE CORNER BRACES STIFFEN THE DOOR FRAME AND ALSO DEFINE THE ARCHED OPENING.

VASILOV, CZECHOSLOVAKIA (1839)

THE WINDOW

THE ANCESTOR OF THE WINDOW IS THE ANCIENT WIND EYE, AN OPENING IN THE ROOF THROUGH WHICH SMOKE COULD ESCAPE.

MUD AND THATCH HUT WITH WIND EYE NORTHERN NIGERIA

ROOF WINDOW FOR LIGHT AND VENTILATION

TAKAYAMA, JAPAN

A VARIETY OF ROOF WINDOWS, OR DORMERS, EVOLVED TO BRING LIGHT AND AIR INTO THE LOFT SPACES.

HAMPSHIRE, ENGLAND

KENT, ENGLAND

HALF DORMER

SAINT AUGUSTINE, FLORIDA (18TH CENTURY)

DORMER WINDOW WITH A HIPPED ROOF

WILLIAMSBURG, VIRGINIA (1730)

DORMER WINDOW IN
A GAMBREL ROOF

WEST MEDFORD,
MASSACHUSETTS
(18th CENTURY)

DORMER WITH
LONG, CATSLIDE ROOF

EPHRATA,
PENNSYLVANIA

HIPPED GABLE ROOF WITH A
SMALL WINDOW IN THE GABLET
TO BRING LIGHT AND AIR
INTO THE LOFT

ENGLAND

EYEBROW WINDOWS
BRING LIGHT AND AIR TO UPPER
LEVEL WITHOUT REQUIRING A FULL-
HEIGHT WALL.

NEW HOPE,
PENNSYLVANIA

UPPER FLOOR

WINDOW

SUNLIGHT

STABLE BELOW

THE ANGLED BARN FLOOR ADMITS
LIGHT TO THE LOWER LEVEL FROM
WINDOWS ABOVE THE
FLOOR TIMBERS.

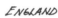

THE PUEBLO INDIANS
SOMETIMES MADE DIAGONAL HOLES AT
THE FLOOR/WALL JUNCTION TO ADMIT
LIGHT TO INTERIOR SPACES.

ZUNI PUEBLO, NEW MEXICO

BUILDERS DISCOVERED VERY QUICKLY
THAT WITH BEVELED JAMBS, A WINDOW OF WIDTH $\underline{x}$
COULD ADMIT MUCH MORE SUNLIGHT (S) ENTERING
AT AN ANGLE.

PRIMITIVE WINDOW WITH
SQUARED JAMBS

MEDIEVAL BEVELED WINDOW

RECESSED WINDOW
WITH ANGLED EXTERIOR
JAMBS AND LINTEL

ALPS

WINDOW WITH ANGLED
INTERIOR JAMBS AND SILL

NEW MEXICO

WEAVER'S WINDOW:

WINDOWS
HAVING ANGLED
STONE AND WOODEN FRAMES ADMIT EXTRA
LIGHT FOR WEAVING.   ENGLAND (1600's)

BEVELED AND
VAULTED INTERIOR
WINDOW FRAME

PENNSYLVANIA

ANGLED JAMBS,
SCALLOPED AND VAULTED TOP,
AND DEEP SILL WITH SEATS

MICHOACAN,
MEXICO

CABIN WALL WITH THE
LOGS BEVELED AT THE WINDOW
TO ADMIT MORE LIGHT

SAVO PROVINCE, FINLAND

PLAN

THE SCALLOPED
RECESSES IN THIS WALL
ALLOW A VIEW TO THE
SIDE FOR PEOPLE-WATCHING
FROM INSIDE.

ARCOS DE LA FRONTERA,
SPAIN

THIS RECESSED WALL BAND
ALLOWS A SIMILAR SIDEWAYS VIEW
THROUGH THE SMALL SECTION OF
GLASS AT THE SIDE OF
THE WINDOW.

SPAIN

METAL GRILLES
GIVE SECURITY
WHILE ADMITTING
LIGHT AND AIR.

GUANAJUATO,
MEXICO

A VARIETY OF WINDOWS WITH
ANGLED JAMBS CREATE INTER-
ESTING LIGHT PATTERNS INSIDE
THIS CHAPEL.

CHAPEL AT RONCHAMP,
FRANCE

THE MOST COMMON DEVICE FOR
PROTECTING THE WINDOW FROM BOTH
WEATHER AND ATTACKERS
IS THE SHUTTER.

BOARD AND BATTEN SHUTTER
BERKS COUNTY,
PENNSYLVANIA

PANEL SHUTTERS
WITH DIAGONAL BOARD
BACKING

PEACH BOTTOM, PENNSYLVANIA

ARCHED PANEL SHUTTERS
COVERING A WINDOW THAT HAS A
VARIETY OF OPENING MODES

SIBERIA

SPLIT SHUTTERS FOR PARTIAL SHADING
ALONG WITH VENTILATION

DEADWOOD, SOUTH DAKOTA

LOUVERED
SLIDING SHUTTERS

NAGASAKI,
JAPAN

HORIZONTALLY HINGED
SHUTTER SET

KAVALLA,
GREECE

HORIZONTALLY HINGED
OUTER SOLID SHUTTER, OR
"SUTOMI," AND INNER TRANS-
LUCENT SHUTTER

JAPAN

INTERIOR SHUTTERS

A BARRED WINDOW
WITH INTERIOR PANEL
SHUTTERS REINFORCED
WITH A BOARD-AND-BATTEN
BACKING AND HAVING A
SMALL INSET DOOR,
OR WICKET, OUT OF
WHICH ONE CAN
PEEK.

SAINT AUGUSTINE, FLORIDA (18ᵗʰ CENTURY)

SECTIONED WINDOW
HAVING SMALL SHUTTERS WITHIN
THE LARGER, FULL-LENGTH,
INTERIOR SHUTTERS

MICHOACÁN, MEXICO

UPPER AND LOWER
BI-FOLD INTERIOR
SHUTTERS

CANTERBURY, NEW HAMPSHIRE
(1811)

SHUTTERS THAT
SLIDE VERTICALLY
FROM BELOW THE
WINDOW

CANTERBURY, NEW HAMPSHIRE
(1831)

DOUBLE SLIDING INDIAN
SHUTTERS, WHICH SLIDE
INTO THE WALL

WILMOT FLAT, NEW HAMPSHIRE
(19ᵗʰ CENTURY)

LOUVERED SHUTTERS
FOR SHADE,
PRIVACY, AND
VENTILATION

ITALY (14ᵗʰ CENTURY)

PENNSYLVANIA
(19ᵗʰ CENTURY)

LATTICEWORK IS WIDELY USED
IN WINDOWS AS A SUNSCREEN
AND TO GIVE SOME
PRIVACY.

WINDOW
WITH GRILLE
AND LATTICE

VENEZUELA

WINDOW WITH
AN ELABORATE WOOD LATTICE

KANAZAWA, JAPAN

THE JAPANESE SHOJI
SCREENS, WHICH ARE COVERED
WITH TRANSLUCENT RICE PAPER,
GIVE PRIVACY WHILE ADMITTING
NATURAL LIGHT.

SHOJI SCREEN
JAPAN

THE TRANSOM ABOVE THIS
WINDOW LETS IN SOME
LIGHT EVEN WHEN
THE SHUTTERS
ARE CLOSED.

HOLLAND

ENCLOSED BALCONY
WITH AWNING WINDOWS ON
THE FRONT AND CASEMENT
WINDOWS ON THE SIDES TO
ALLOW GREATER FLEXIBILITY
TO MEET DIFFERENT
WEATHER CONDITIONS

VALETTA, MALTA

THE UPPER SASH
OF THIS SECOND-
FLOOR WINDOW
PIVOTS FOR GOOD
AIR FLOW AND
EASY CLEANING.

CUMBRIA, ENGLAND

THE POINTED UPPER SASH
EXTENDS THIS DOUBLE HUNG
WINDOW UP INTO THE
TRIANGULAR ARCH.

CUMBRIA, ENGLAND

THIS TILTED
DOUBLE HUNG
WINDOW BRINGS
LIGHT IN THROUGH
THE SMALL WALL
AREA BETWEEN
THE ROOFS.

GRANTHAM,
NEW HAMPSHIRE

CORNER WINDOW
HOLLAND

COMBINATION OF WICKET (WINDOW WITHIN A WINDOW) AND CASEMENT WINDOWS WITH VERTICALLY AND HORIZONTALLY HINGED SHUTTERS

SWITZERLAND

THICK WALLS ALLOW THE WINDOWS TO BE RECESSED EITHER FROM THE OUTSIDE FOR WEATHER PROTECTION OR FROM THE INSIDE TO CREATE A SEAT OR A SHELF.

DEEP SILL WITH A WINDOW SEAT

PENNSYLVANIA

SILL SHELF

CZECHOSLOVAKIA

WINDOW TRACKS HELD ONLY WITH THUMBSCREWS ALLOW EASY REMOVAL OF SASH FOR CLEANING.

NEW HAMPSHIRE

A TRANSOM SIMPLIFIES THE BUILDING PROCESS BY PUTTING A DOOR AND A WINDOW UNDER ONE LINTEL.

NEW YORK

THIS SMALL WINDOW WAS PLACED IN THE ROOF TO BRING NATURAL LIGHT TO THE STAIRWAY AND HALL.

PENNSYLVANIA

THE STAIRWAY

SINCE PALEOLITHIC
TIMES SIMPLE STAIRWAYS
HAVE BEEN BUILT BY
CHOPPING A SERIES OF
NOTCHES INTO
LONG LOGS.

SALISH UNDERGROUND
TRIBAL BUILDING

CANADA

NORWEGIAN
LOG STAIR

TWIN NOTCHED LOGS
WITH STAIR TREADS
BETWEEN

NOTCHED
TIMBER LADDER
WITH HAND RUNGS

PENNSYLVANIA

LASHED LADDER FOR
ROOF ENTRANCE
TO PUEBLO DWELLING

TAOS, NEW MEXICO

LADDER STAIR
WITH HANDRAIL

KANAZAWA, JAPAN

LADDER THAT
SWINGS DOWN FROM
BETWEEN CEILING
JOISTS

CANTERBURY,
NEW HAMPSHIRE

BUILDERS IN MANY
AREAS HAVE CHOSEN
TO PUT THE STAIRWAY
ON THE OUTSIDE OF
THE STRUCTURE TO
SAVE THE LIMITED
INTERIOR SPACE.

IRON AGE "CHIPURO" SHELTER
APULIA, ITALY

STONE HOUSE

LEMNOS, GREECE

STAIRWAY OF
STONES PROJECTING
FROM A MASONRY
WALL

SWITZERLAND

STEPS OF
CUT STONE BLOCKS

FRANCE

EXTERNAL STAIR-
WAYS ARE ESPECIALLY
POPULAR IN WARMER
CLIMATES.

INTERTWINING
NETWORK OF
STAIRWAYS

SPERLONGA, ITALY

THIS ARCHED
STAIRWAY HAS A
RAMP FOR PACK
DONKEYS BESIDE
STEPS FOR PEOPLE
AND LEADS UP
TO A TANK ROOM
ABOVE THE
CISTERNS.

GUANAJUATO, MEXICO

YEARS OF REPEATED WHITE-
WASHING GRADUALLY SOFTEN
THE SHARP ANGLE AT WHICH
WALL AND STEP MEET.

SIENA,
ITALY

STEPPED
PEDESTRIAN RAMP
ALONGSIDE A STAIRWAY
LEADING TO A BALCONY
CROSSWALK

MYKONOS,
GREECE

A STILE LETS PEOPLE
CROSS A FENCE BUT KEEPS LIVE-
STOCK IN, AND IT IS MUCH
EASIER TO USE THAN A GATE,
ESPECIALLY WHEN CARRYING
SOMETHING.

EPHRATA,
PENNSYLVANIA

ARCHED ADOBE
STAIRWAY WITH
STORAGE BELOW

SAN ANTONIO,
TEXAS
(19th CENTURY)

DOWN →

CONTEMPORARY SPIRAL STAIRWAY
WITH DOUBLE TURN

NEW LONDON, NEW HAMPSHIRE

SPIRAL STAIRWAY SCULPTED BY
WHARTON ESHRICK USING TENONED OAK
LOG TREADS AND DRIFTWOOD RAILINGS

PAOLI, PENNSYLVANIA

STAIRWAY WITH
STORAGE DRAWERS

RICHTERSWIL,
SWITZERLAND
(CA. 1756)

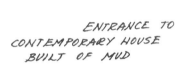

ENTRANCE TO
CONTEMPORARY HOUSE
BUILT OF MUD

BUILDING SYSTEMS

UNITIZED ROOF
FOR EASY CONSTRUCTION
AND TRANSPORTATION
TO THE SITE

THIS STRUCTURAL ROOF PANEL
IS BUILT ON THE GROUND, BY
LASHING TOGETHER PALM LEAF RIBS,
AND THEN HOISTED UP
AND THATCHED.

DETAIL OF
LASHING

SEE
DETAIL

CAMEROON

IN TIMBER FRAMING,
WHOLE WALL SECTIONS,
OR BENTS, ARE
ASSEMBLED ON THE
GROUND, TILTED
INTO POSITION,
BRACED, AND THEN
FRAMED INTO THE
OTHER BENTS.

UNIONVILLE, PENNSYLVANIA

FORM BOARDS HAVE BEEN USED
OVER THE CENTURIES AS MOLDS FOR
BUILDING WALLS OF MUD, TABBY
(SEE PAGE 103), PACKED EARTH,
STONES (SEE PAGE 131), AND
CONCRETE.

FORM
BOARD

BRACE

SHOJI

FUSUMA

TATAMI

BATH

WC

KITCHEN
(WOOD FLOOR)

IN TRADITIONAL JAPANESE
HOUSES, THE FLOOR PLAN, SHOJIS,
AND FUSUMAS ALL FOLLOW A
MODULAR GRID BASED ON THE
TATAMI MAT (SEE PAGE 132).

EXPANSION

THE INTUITIVE, CIRCULAR FORM OF THE NEOLITHIC BEEHIVE HUT (RIGHT) PRECLUDES THE SIMPLE EXPANSION OF THE INTERIOR SPACE,

BUT THE RATIONAL, RECTANGULAR FORM OFFERS THE POSSIBILITY OF EASY, LINEAR GROWTH (LEFT).

CARIB INDIAN STRUCTURE, GUIANA

ANOTHER WAY TO EXPAND A DWELLING IS TO BUILD ADDITIONAL UNITS THAT INTERFACE WITH THE EXISTING STRUCTURE.

HOUSE COMPOUND CAMEROON

VERTICAL GROWTH, AS IN THE TERMITE MOUND (ABOVE), IS ANOTHER EFFECTIVE MODE OF EXPANSION.

(CA. 1710)

(CA. 1750)

THE EARLY HOUSES OF ST. AUGUSTINE, FLORIDA WERE OFTEN EXPANDED VERTICALLY BY ADDING ANOTHER FLOOR ABOVE THE TABBY-WALLED FIRST FLOOR.

OTHER COMMON EXPANSION TECHNIQUES ARE THE LEAN-TO (LEFT) AND THE EL (RIGHT).

RHODE ISLAND

VERMONT

MOBILE ARCHITECTURE

TEPEE COVER

TRAVOIS

THE TRAVOIS, DRAWN BY HORSES AFTER THEIR INTRODUCTION BY THE SPANISH, USUALLY CONSISTED OF TEPEE POLES BETWEEN WHICH THE TEPEE COVER (LEFT) WAS CARRIED WITH VARIOUS BELONGINGS.

THE WALL PANELS OF MANY YURTS COLLAPSE LIKE A SCISSORS GATE FOR EASY TRANSPORTATION.

WALL OF MONGUL YURT

THE LARGE BEDOUIN TENTS ARE MADE TO BE EASILY CARRIED BY CAMELS.

THE BOW-TOP ENGLISH GYPSY VAN HAS PROVISIONS FOR SLEEPING, COOKING, EATING, AND SITTING WHILE TRAVELING, AND IT PROTECTS AGAINST BAD WEATHER.

PLAN OF GYPSY VAN

BULGARIAN SLEIGH HUT

THE WOOD AND WATTLE-AND-DAUB SLEIGH HUTS OF THE BULGARIAN NOMADIC SHEPHERDS ARE LARGE ENOUGH TO HOUSE ENTIRE FAMILIES.

BARGE
HOUSEBOAT

AMSTERDAM,
HOLLAND

WHETHER BECAUSE OF LIMITED AVAILABLE
LAND OR TOO HIGH A PRICE FOR IT, PEOPLE IN
MANY PARTS OF THE WORLD HAVE CHOSEN TO LIVE
ON THE WATER IN EVERYTHING FROM CONVERTED
BARGES TO DWELLINGS BUILT ON
ARTIFICIAL ISLANDS.

FLOATING
VILLAGE BUILT
ON A PLATFORM
OF BAMBOO

YELLOW RIVER, CHINA
(CA. 1668)

THE CHINESE EMPEROR WU-TI
(140-86 B.C.) HAD A FLOATING WOODEN
FORTRESS THAT MEASURED 600 FEET ON
A SIDE AND GARRISONED 2,000
MEN PLUS THEIR HORSES.

Bibliography

Allen, Edward. *Stone Shelters*. Cambridge, Mass.: MIT Press, 1969.

Anderson, Cardwell. "Primitive Shelter." *AIA Journal* (October and November, 1961).

*Arthur, Eric, and Dudley Witney. *The Barn*. Greenwich, Conn.: New York Graphic Society Books, 1972.

*Baldwin, J., and Stewart Brand. *Soft Tech*. New York: Penguin Books, 1978.

*Bemis, A. F., and J. Burchard. *The Evolving House*. Cambridge, Mass.: Tech Press, 1931.

Broderick, Alan Haughton. "Grass Roots." *Architectural Review* (London) 686 (February 1954).

Bunting, Bainbridge. *Early Architecture in New Mexico*. Albuquerque: University of Mexico Press, 1976.

Butti, Ken, and John Perlin. *A Golden Thread*. Palo Alto, Cal.: Chesire Books, 1980.

*Camesasca, Ettore. *History of the House* (first American edition). New York: Putnam, 1971.

Carver, Norman F., Jr. *Italian Hilltowns*. Kalamazoo, Mich.: Documan Press, 1979.

*Chamberlain, Samuel. *Domestic Architecture in Rural France*. New York: Architectural Book Publishing Co., Inc., 1981.

*Currant, William, and Vincent Skully. *Pueblo Architecture of the Southwest*. Austin: University of Texas Press, 1971.

*Dupont, Jean-Claude. *Habitation Rurale au Québec*. Montreal: Cahiers du Québec/Hurtubise HMH, 1978.

Fitch, James Marston. *American Building 2: The Environmental Forces that Shape It*. Boston: Houghton Mifflin, 1972.

Fitch, James Marston. "Primitive Architecture." *Scientific American* (December 1960).

Fletcher, Sir Bannister. *A History of Architecture on the Comparative Method*. New York: Charles Scribner's Sons, 1975.

Foley, Mary Mix. *The American House*. New York: Harper Colophon Books, 1980.

*von Frisch, Karl. *Animal Architecture*. New York: Harcourt Brace Jovanovich, 1974.

*Futagawa, Yukio. *Villages and Towns* (vols. 1, 3, 5, 6, 8, 9). Tokyo: Ada Edita, 1973.

*Futagawa, Yukio. *Wooden Houses*. New York: Abrams, 1979.

Gardi, René. *Indigenous African Architecture*. New York: van Nostrand Reinhold Co., 1973.

*Gardiner, Stephen. *Evolution of the House*. London: Constable, 1975.

*Gasparini, Graziano. *La Casa Colonial Venezolana*. Caracas: Universidad Central de Venezuela, 1962.

Gay, Larry. *Heating With Wood*. Charlotte, Vt.: Garden Way Publishing Co., 1974.

Givoni, B. *Man, Climate and Architecture* (second edition). New York: van Nostrand Reinhold, 1981.

Glassie, Henry. *Fold Housing in Middle Virginia*. Knoxville: University of Tennessee Press, 1975.

*Grillo, P. J. *What Is Design?* Chicago: University of Chicago Press, 1960.

*Gropp, Louis. *48 Energy Saving Designs*. New York: Pantheon, 1978.

*Gschwend, Fehlman, and Hunziker. *Ballenberg: The Swiss Open-Air Museum*. Aarau, Switzerland: AT Verlag, 1982.

*Hubrecht, R. and G. Doyon. *L'Architecture Rurale et Bourgeoise en France*. Paris: Vincent, Freal & Co., 1942.

Kahn, Lloyd, ed. *Shelter*. Bolinas, Cal.: Shelter Publications, 1973.

Kahn, Lloyd, ed. *Shelter II*. Bolinas, Cal.: Shelter Publications, 1978.

*Kennedy, Robert Woods. *The House and the Art of its Design*. New York: Reinhold, 1953.

*Kinzey, B. Y., and H. M. Sharp. *Environmental Technologies in Architecture*. Englewood Cliffs, N.J.: Prentice-Hall, Inc., 1951.

*Knowles, Ralph L. *Energy and Form*. Cambridge, Mass.: MIT Press, 1974.

*Konstantinidas, N. Aris. *Elements for Self-Knowledge*. Athens, 1975.

Manucy, Albert. *The Houses of St. Augustine, 1565-1821*. Tallahassee, Fla.: Rose Printing Co., 1962.

*Means, P. A. *Ancient Civilizations of the Andes*. New York: Charles Scribner's Sons, 1931.

*Megas, St. "Studies in Folk Architecture." *Laographia*, vol. 26. Athens: Society of Hellenic Laography, 1969.

Mercer, Eric. *English Vernacular Houses*. London: H. M. Stationery Office, 1975.

*Moholy-Nagy, Sibyl. *Native Genius in Anonymous Architecture*. New York: Horizon Press, 1957.

*Morgan, Lewis H. *Houses and House Life of the American Aborigines*. Chicago: University of Chicago Press, 1965.

Morse, Edward S. *Japanese Homes and their Surroundings*. New York: Dover Publications, 1961.

*Olgyay, Victor. *Design with Climate*. Princeton: Princeton University Press, 1963.

Olgyay, Aladar, and Victor Olgyay. *Solar Control and Shading Devices*. Princeton: Princeton University Press, 1957.

*Oliver, Paul. *Shelter in Africa*. New York: Praeger, 1971.

Oliver, Paul. *Shelter, Sign and Symbol*. Woodstock, N.Y.: Overlook Press, 1977.

Parker, John Henry. *A Concise Glossary of Architecture*. London: Parke & Co., 1882.

Penoyre, John, and Jayne Penoyre. *Houses in the Landscape*. Boston: Faber and Faber, 1978.

*Rapoport, Amos. *House, Form and Culture*. Englewood Cliffs, N.J.: Prentice-Hall, 1969.

*Raymond, Eleanor. *Early Domestic Architecture of Pennsylvania*. New York: Wm. Helburn, Inc., 1931.

*Rivière, G. H. *Maisons de Bois*. Paris: Centre Georges Pompidou, 1979.

*Robinson, David M. *Excavations at Olynthus: The Hellenic House*. Baltimore: Johns Hopkins Press, 1938.

Rudofsky, Bernard. *Architecture Without Architects*. New York: Doubleday & Co., Inc., 1964.

*Rudofsky, Bernard. *Now I Lay Me Down to Eat*. New York: Anchor Press (Doubleday), 1980.

*Rudofsky, Bernard. *The Prodigious Builders*. New York: Harcourt Brace Jovanovich, 1977.

*Safdie, Moshe. *Form and Purpose*. Boston: Houghton Mifflin, 1982.

*Schoenauer, Norbert. *6,000 Years of Housing*, vols. 1, 2, 3. New York: Garland STMP Press, 1981.

Sergeant, John. *Frank Lloyd Wright's Usonian Houses*. New York: Watson-Guptill Publications, 1975.

*Severin, Timothy. *Vanishing Primitive Man*. New York: American Heritage Publishing Co., 1973.

*Shipway, Verna Cook, and Warren Shipway. *The Mexican House: Old and New*. New York: Architectural Book Publishing Co., 1960.

*Skurka, Norma, and John Naar. *Design for a Limited Planet*. New York: Ballantine Books, 1976.

*Sloane, Eric. *An Age of Barns*. New York: Ballantine Books, 1967.

Sloane, Eric. *A Reverence for Wood*. New York: Funk and Wagnalls, 1965.

Sprigg, June. *By Shaker Hands*. New York: Alfred A. Knopf, Inc., 1975.

*Weslager, C. A. *The Log Cabin in America*. New Brunswick, N.J.: Rutgers University Press, 1969.

*Zook, Nicholas. *Museum Villages of the U.S.A.* Barre, Mass.: Barre Publishing, 1971.

---

*Indicates books that are out of print.

Index